A Tale of Two Sisters :
Lives of Travel and Adventure

Anne Harden

Cybercom Publishing
Toronto

A Tale of Two Sisters: A Tale of Travel and Adventure
Copyright © 2002 by Cybercom Publishing

All rights reserved. No part of this book may be used or reproduced, stored in a retrieval system, or transmitted in any form by any means, photocopying, electronic, mechanical, recording or otherwise without the prior written permission of the copyright holder except in the case of brief quotations embodied in reviews.

This edition published in 2002 by
Cybercom Publishing
394 Woodsworth Rd., Unit # 50,
Toronto, Ontario, Canada M2L 2T9.
e-mail: publisher@cybercominc.net

Cover, layout and text design: Tim Harrison
Editor: Roger Muller
Printed and bound in the United States of America
and London, England

Care has been taken to trace the ownership of any copyright material contained in this text. The publisher will gladly accept any information that will enable them to rectify any reference or credit in subsequent editions.

National Library of Canada Cataloguing in Publication

**Harden, Anne, 1922-
A tale of two sisters / Anne Harden.**

**Includes index.
ISBN 0-9731925-0-X**

1. Harden, Anne, 1922- 2. Harden, Sheila. 3. Harden family. 4. World War, 1939-1945--Personal narratives, British. 5. Diplomats--Great Britain--Biography. 6. London (England)--Biography. I. Title.

DA566.9.H287A3 2002   940.54'8141   C2002 905109-6

Dedicated with love and gratitude

To Sheila

And to my father and mother

Jo and Eanswythe

Table of Contents

1	Prelude	5
2	Ancestry	7
3	Childhood	17
4	Education and Travel in Continental Europe	22
5	Ceylon	39
6	War in Ceylon	45
7	Buddha's Rays	53
8	The Most Dangerous Moment of the War	57
9	The Post Raid Period	67
10	The Last of the Raj	73
11	Tragedy	79
12	Returning to England	83
13	The War in England	86
14	Post-War Years	96
15	The Oxford University Press	101
16	Some Travel Stories	109
17	Sheila enters the Foreign Service	113
18	Sheila in the Diplomatic Service	116
19	Travels in the Americas	126
20	Micronesia	132
21	Epilogue	139
A1	Acknowledgements	146
A2	Illustrations	147

1

Prelude

It was early in March 1938 that streaks of glaring lights appeared over the Nordkette, the great range that divides Austria from Germany. 'It's the invasion,' cried out the local peasants and sent fire engines thinking the frontier was breached. 'No' said my father a retired naval commander, 'it's just the Northern Lights.' He had seen them often when cruising in North Atlantic waters, but it was very unusual for them to be sighted as far south as the Austrian Tyrol. An omen perhaps!

A few days later on 13 March we awoke in the little Gasthaus the Jagerhof, to find Hitler had indeed invaded Austria during the night. We had been living there intermittently during the last four years, while my elder sister, Sheila, and I were being educated, and after my father's job as Harbour Master in Port Sudan had ended. This had followed his retirement from the Royal Navy in 1932. At breakfast a stout German ex-officer appeared proudly displaying his World War I medals. The sinister Third Reich had absorbed Austria.

I remember that morning we all went for a walk down the valley - the Stubaital - to Fulpmes, when suddenly German soldiers on motorcycles passed us. By midday every schoolchild even in this remote valley, had been given a swastika armlet and every non-Nazi schoolteacher or official had been replaced.

Next day we drove down to Innsbruck, which was about fifteen miles away. My father went to see the British Consul to find out whether we should leave the country. Lovely Innsbruck, which we had known so well during the four years we had spent in Austria, was transformed. Innsbruck, which we had visited for treats to eat splendid cakes at Schindlers in the Maria Theresienstrasse and drink hot chocolate under layers of cream, or visit the Hofkirche, was changed. German bombers were circling the city almost at rooftop height intimidating the inhabitants, people were weeping in the shops and there was fear. This was the first time I had seen the new horrific side of Germany. I was fifteen.

2

Ancestry

My father's family the Hardens, come from the squirearchy of Northern Ireland. Staunch Orangemen, they had been settled there at least since the Battle of the Boyne, when an ancestor was given the land, called Harrybrook, for his services to King William III. Probably the family originated on the Scottish border, or some sources suggest they were Huguenots fleeing the France of Louis XIV, after the Revocation of the Edict of Nantes in 1685. However, as all records were burned in Dublin in the 1922 Troubles, it is difficult to trace them back before 1740 when a Harden of Harrybrook was a JP. My grandfather George as the youngest son, joined the army retiring as Lt. Colonel of the Royal Sussex Regiment. As a young officer he had fought in the Sudan, despite the heat still wearing a scarlet uniform. He took part in the unsuccessful and belated forced march sent to relieve General Gordon in Khartoum, who was surrounded by the forces of the Mahdi.

It was a formidable task facing the commanding officer, General Sir Garnet Wolseley. It was twelve hundred miles from Cairo to Khartoum and the Nile had four huge cataracts barring their way. Time too was running out. Undeterred he had hundreds of whaleboats constructed and specially supervised by Canadian voyageurs, who were used to such waters. The boats had to be hauled and portaged up these raging waters. But at the top, the Nile made a huge loop northeast. He decided to send a desert column mounted on camels, across the desert, which would halve the time to reach Khartoum. This force, which consisted of only 1,800 men (including my grandfather), was led by the charismatic Colonel Stewart. On 17 January 10,000 Dervishes at Abu Klea attacked them. Churchill described the battle as 'the most savage and bloody action ever fought in the Sudan.' The Dervishes lost 1,100 men and the British 74 killed and 94 wounded. However, the fighting was not over. Stewart realized that the Mahdi's forces were regrouping and he prepared thorn hedges to defend his column. He won the subsequent battle but was mortally wounded. The column reached the Nile on 21 January. The command was taken over by Sir Charles Wilson, who decided to rest the men for three days. It was fatal. When they arrived at Khartoum on 28 January they were two days too late. The colours of Islam had replaced the Union flag. 50,000 dervishes had overwhelmed Khartoum and Gordon was murdered on the steps of his palace. The Sudan was not to be recaptured by General Kitchener for another ten years.

My paternal grandfather was then posted to India where he met and married my grandmother Mabel Angelo. The Angelos were an extremely colourful family and as my great-uncle Cecil had dug into family history as I have, much more is known about them and their antecedents. The family was originally called Malevolti Tremamondo - the Malevolti coming from one of the great families of Siena and the Tremamondos from rich merchants of Leghorn. Domenico Angelo (he soon dropped the Italian names) came to England in the eighteenth century and founded a famous fencing academy in Soho. He also taught both riding and fencing to George III and George IV when they were Princes of Wales.

Mr. Henry Angelo's Fencing Academy, 1787: Thomas Rowlandson, (Cecil Higgins Art Gallery, Bedford)

The family flourished and sent its sons to join the East India Company's army. One ancestor was a great friend of Warren Hastings. A later Angelo married a Van Cortlandt girl. Her family was even more rewarding to investigate. The Van Cortlandts had emigrated to New York, when it was a Dutch colony in the seventeenth century and set up vast estates along the Hudson. Stefanus Van Cortlandt was the first native born Mayor or Burgomaster, of New York in 1677. Van Cortlandt houses can still be seen on the Hudson and in New York City. When the War of Independence broke out, my ancestor Philip Van Cortlandt fought for King George III. His manor house in Hanover, New Jersey was requisitioned by Washington's troops and his family treated 'in a manner that would disgrace the most savage Barbarians.' His wife and eleven children were then turned out in a snowstorm. He himself had made a perilous escape to join the royal army. However, Washington seems to have relented, because I found the original pass signed by General Washington in the Public Record Office, allowing Mrs Van Cortlandt and her large family to pass through the enemy lines and rejoin her husband in Yorktown. Here the war was lost and the United States came into being.

For twenty years Philip and his family travelled to Canada, the West Indies and eventually arrived in England. Endless petitions were written by Philip asking for compensation for the loss of his lands and fortune, through his loyalty to King George. Meanwhile his uncle Pierre Van Cortlandt took his property. He became first Lieutenant Governor of the State of New York under the United States.

In England Philip's plea for compensation was eventually granted by Parliament. He was given a pension, commissions in the navy and army for his sons mainly in the Indian army, and dowries for his daughters. It was Philip's grandson, Major Frederick Angelo, whose three children were all involved in the Indian Mutiny. They were John Angelo, my great-grandfather, Mary and Frederick.

John fought under John Nicholson and held the dying general in his arms at Delhi Gate when the city was recaptured. Mary who was married to Sir Richard Oldfield a judge, had taken refuge in Agra at the outbreak of the Mutiny. He gallantly led a sortie to beat off the besiegers, but sadly two of their small children died from the diseases rampant in the fortress. Meanwhile Lieutenant Frederick Angelo had been appointed to Cawnpore. He was now married to Helena - they had two small daughters and she was expecting another child. According to family history his Indian servant warned him that trouble was brewing. Wisely he secretly sent his family down river hidden under rugs to Allahabad.

In 1956 I discovered roughly pasted into an old family photo album, which had once belonged to the younger of Frederick's two little girls Cousin Katie, pages from a faded diary dated 1857. This diary had never been read. It was difficult to decipher, as apart from the faintness of the ink, it was interspersed with foreign words. However, with the help of an ex-Indian army friend, (Alec Halliley who had married my friend Rosemary Ogilvie) who knew Urdu, and by research in the India Office Library and elsewhere, I was able to transcribe it. I subsequently published the diary in *Notes and Queries*. It was fascinating reading, as poor Helena described very vividly, her escape down river to Allahabad and, eventually to Calcutta through the mutinous country. At Allahabad the children became ill, the colonel's wife was difficult, the Mutiny broke out there too and on every page Helena was wondering what had happened to Fred. She had need to worry. Frederick was captured at the fall of the cantonment, which had become untenable - no food or ammunition - but they were offered safe conduct by Nana Sahib. Instead, they were shot down in the small boats transporting them across the river. Those men that survived were murdered and the women and children taken to Cawnpore and, just before the rescue army arrived, were butchered and thrown down a well, some of them were not even dead. It was the worst crime of the Mutiny and the retaliations that followed caused bitterness that was to last. Meanwhile Helena and her small daughters escaped down river to Calcutta and safety with Elliott Angelo, her brother-in-law. Sadly, Frederick's posthumous son Frederick was killed twenty years later in an Afghan War.

My mother's family the Rentons, came from Fife and the borders of Scotland and intermarried with the Wemysses, Homes, Leslies, and Douglases. My great-grandfather, John Renton was a Presbyterian minister and headmaster of a school in Auchtermuchtie. A brilliant classical scholar, his eight children seem to have been equally clever, one becoming one of Scotland's top surgeons, another (I think) Advocate-General, and my grandfather Alexander, who added his godfather's rather dull name Wood to his surname, Renton a judge, and eventually Chief Justice of Ceylon (now Sri Lanka) and later Treasurer of Gray's Inn. His judgments are still used to this day in Sri Lanka.

Granddaddy Renton died when I was only nine, but Sheila and I loved him dearly. He was a wonderful storyteller and when I stayed with my grandparents in Kensington, I would go down to his study in the early morning and he would enthrall me with stories of some of his cases. One in particular I remember. There were two rich Singhalese sisters, who lived with their brother in Colombo. One day he was stabbed to death. One of their servants, a child of about nine, admitted to the crime and her fingerprints were found on the dagger. Each day as the trial progressed, the two sisters appearing as witnesses, arrived in different and more beguiling saris. Then the little girl gave her testimony. My grandfather the judge, complimented her and asked her to repeat her statement. This she did, repeating word for word what she had already said. She had obviously been coached. Under skilful cross-examination she revealed that the two sisters had held her hand, forcing her to kill their brother as he slept. They hoped to inherit his large fortune. Instead they faced the gallows.

My mother was called Eanswythe. This unusual name was chosen by my grandfather, who when she was born, had recently been converted to High Anglicanism. He was interested in the newly discovered bones of this obscure Anglo-Saxon saint, granddaughter of King Ethelbert of Kent. My great-grandmother born Janet Wemyss, must have been nervous of his changing denominations, as she refused to allow him to study at Oxford then the centre of the Oxford Movement, and sent him to Edinburgh instead. However, all to no avail, as once at Gray's Inn where he became a barrister, he came under the influence of Father Stanton a noted perpetual curate at St Alban's Holborn, and became an Anglican. At least, not a follower of 'The Scarlet Woman' of my great-grandmother's fears!

Mother spent her early childhood in Mauritius, where Granddaddy was Advocate-General. She was aged four at the time. They travelled there in a French ship. My mother remembered how each day, when she was taken to visit all the sheep and pigs, their numbers had diminished. There were no refrigerators in 1901, at least not in their ship, and the nice animals were eaten in turn! In Mauritius the family lived with the Governor, Sir Charles Bruce and his wife. Lady Bruce was devoted to my mother, perhaps because her only son had been killed as a young man, rescuing the body of the Prince Imperial, who had been ambushed and killed by tribesmen in Africa. On my mother's fifth birthday Lady Bruce insisted that my mother, as a treat should dine with the household and guests. At that period a governor's dinner was a long, grand and stately occasion with the gentlemen leading in the ladies. Sir Charles took my mother's tiny hand - she was small for her age - and proceeded with her to the seat of honour. When it came to the Loyal Toast, they all rose to their feet and Sir Charles gruffly announced 'His Majesty the King!' and Lady Bruce piped in 'and baby too!'

Just before the First World War my grandfather was appointed to Ceylon as Chief Justice, his family accompanying him. Actually my mother went at a later date, as she was at school in Paris learning French. She remembered how in July 1914, two of the girls one an Austrian, who they all liked, and one a Serb, who they disliked, began quarrelling violently over the murder of to them, an unknown archduke. Little did they realize that the assassination of the Austrian Archduke Franz Ferdinand was the immediate cause of the nightmare of the First World War!

My mother spent the next three years in Ceylon, having already been there a year before, when she was fourteen. She often travelled with my grandfather when he went on circuit in jungle areas and to the north of the island. There were times of unrest and on one occasion, on the way to his court, their car was halted by a dangerous mob. Mother admitted that she was very frightened, but my grandfather a small man, but one of the few people I have met who did not know the meaning of fear (he said it was not courage as he was unafraid), got out of the car, and faced the angry demonstrators ordering them not to hinder the rule of justice. They melted away.

When they were camping in the jungle my mother would entertain the company with romantic songs, accompanying herself on her guitar. Though no musician, she had a delightful singing voice. Most of the officials at that time were British, but many of the puisne judges were Ceylonese, mostly Singhalese, but some called Burghers, were descendants of the Portuguese or Dutch colonial rulers and Singhalese women. Unlike the impression one might gain from many books written about the Raj my grandparents and other white officials constantly entertained them in their houses, though clubs were segregated until Independence.

While my mother was in Ceylon, my father George, (called Jo by his friends), came on leave to Ceylon from Mesopotamia. He had joined the Royal Navy at fourteen in the last of the 'terms' in the old training ship the *Britannia* and passed for Lieutenant with six "firsts" in 1909. After serving in various ships, he was sent to Turkish ruled Mesopotamia, modern Iraq, as navigator in the gunboat *Espiègle*, one of a small flotilla under the command of Captain Wilfrid Nunn (later Vice-Admiral), just before the outbreak of the First World War. He remembered how Turkish officials in August 1914 came on an official visit to the Odin. The captain offered them a drink and to his dismay being Moslems, they asked for sherbet. Knowing there was none in the ship, he nevertheless, summoned his steward and ordered sherbet. In a few minutes pink drinks appeared and eventually the guests left. Later the captain asked his steward how he had obtained the sherbet. The steward replied, 'Well sir I knew it was pink and fizzy, so I mixed your pink toothpaste with Eno's fruit salts.' War with Turkey was declared shortly afterwards!

I think it is often forgotten how much the success of our armies, escorted by the small British gunboats, which sailed up and down the Tigris and Euphrates guarding them, led to the final surrender of Turkey on 31 October 1918, twelve days before the main Armistice on 11 November. All people mostly remember is the disastrous Dardanelles campaign and the capture of Kut.

Captain Nunn describes the reasons for the war in this area in his authoritative book *Tigris Gunboats*: 'Very soon after the outbreak of the War it became apparent that Turkey might be drawn into the vortex on the side of Germany, and British local interests jeopardized thereby. With Turkey hostile moreover, enemy interest and propaganda would soon spread throughout Persia, thence to Afghanistan and the unruly tribes of the Indian Northwest Frontier. Again the possibility of Basra becoming a hostile port, improved by the Germans and connected to Central Europe by the Baghdad Railway, which might well convey the material and personnel for a submarine base, from which our Indian sea communications could be preyed upon, would not bear contemplation.'

The gunboats moved up the Tigris, supporting the army, and captured immense numbers of Turks and their Arab allies. Daddy told me years later that at one point he and two able seamen had taken two hundred prisoners with hardly a fight. At this early stage, before the Germans and more experienced Turkish officers took over, the Turks seemed anxious to become prisoners. Once when he was in charge of a boatload of them, he lost the way in the dark among the shoals of the river. However, a Turkish officer tapped the coxswain on the back and pointed the correct way! They were keen to get to Basra and the comforts of the good food with which they knew the British provided their prisoners!

But then Germany and Turkey replaced their commanders. 'The Mesopotamian picnic was over'.

My father took part in the capture of Kurna, the strongholds of Amara and Kut. He also helped to chase and seize the Turkish gunboat the *Marmariss*. All this time he was as navigator, being sent to sound the narrow river ahead and its obstacles, such as sunken ships or flotsam, while under heavy fire. The weather in mid summer was almost unbearable and one Tommy was heard to remark that if this really was the site of the Garden of Eden 'it wouldn't have needed an angel with a flaming sword to keep him out!'

Major-General Townshend (afterwards Sir C.V.F Townshend) arrived from India to take command of the Tigris operations. He had made his name twenty-four years before against the wild Pathans in India. He was a highly skilled commander and a born fighter. He outfought and out-generalled the Turks to take Kut, but then he wished to push on to the ultimate goal of Baghdad. He believed that his 6th Division from India, 'could storm the gates of hell.' Earl Haig categorized him as 'a semi-lunatic' and King George V 'as an advertising sort of fellow'. However, he was heavily defeated outside Kut and forced to retreat into the city. He was highly criticized for the campaign but it is for military experts to judge him.

The gunboat flotilla was way beyond Kut when the army began its retreat.
The three gunboats, the *Firefly*, the *Comet*, and the *Sumana* were under heavy gunfire as they were the last ships to leave the stricken city, which fell on 29 April. The *Comet* repeatedly hit, was soon ablaze and her crew evacuated to the Sumana. The *Firefly* was aground with Turkish troops advancing for her capture, but her crew was still on board. My father volunteered, taking with him, Seaman Guy, to row back, under constant fire, to rescue them (and the confidential books). For this action he was awarded the DSO for gallantry and Guy the DSM.

After valiant attempts to relieve Kut both by the army and navy, the city surrendered on 29 April 1916 and close to 12,000 officers and men (including General Towshend) were captured after a heroic defence lasting 147 days. 70% of the British and 30% of the Indian officers and men of those imprisoned, died in the appalling prisons to which they were taken. The Turks lost 10,000 men. It was the worst disaster suffered by the British army between Yorktown in 1781 and Singapore in 1942.

But what is so often forgotten, Kut was retaken in February 1917 and it was Captain Nunn who rehoisted the Union Jack over the city. Our triumphant army with new commanders, and the ever-watchful gunboats (including my father's) advanced up the Tigris and captured the all-important city of Baghdad on 11 March. An officer of the 14th Hussars wrote: 'Baghdad, the goal towards which we have been looking for so long, sometimes with hope very often with some doubt. But here we were and we realized that with our presence one pan-German dream was shattered and that the Union Jack and not the German Eagle soared over the City of the Caliphs.'

General Marshall continued the campaign routing the Turks at Mosul. Meanwhile General Allenby had entered Jerusalem. The Middle East was in Allied hands.

During his time in Mespot, as it was always called, daddy went on leave to Ceylon: My father, along with other officers was invited to the Wood Renton house and there met, and fell in love with my mother. It was a love that lasted all their lives. She at that time though only seventeen, was engaged to a high-flying civil servant, who eventually became a Colonial Governor. He was twenty years older than my mother and she was already getting bored with him and his much older friends. She broke off their engagement.

My mother who was always rather psychic, had a strange experience in the Galle Face Hotel in Colombo, which is still there. While granddaddy was on circuit over the New Year of 1917, she was sharing the main suite with granny, who was nervous of sleeping alone. They had left the revellers about midnight, but my mother had not yet gone to sleep, when she heard the door open. In the dim light she saw the figure of a man move towards the window, which looked out over the *maidan* (green), that divides the hotel from the town of Colombo. She thought it must be a fellow guest, who perhaps a bit drunk, had come into the wrong room. He moved across to the window and as he did so, the lighthouse that stands in the middle of the town came on. It went right through his body and she realized that she was seeing only a shadow. He now moved towards her bed and began pressing down on her mosquito net. Terrified she screamed for granny to put on the light, which she did. There was nothing there. Her first thought was 'I mustn't tell mother that there's a ghost in the room!' 'Sorry,' she said, 'I must have had a nightmare.' She got up but they had locked the door. They later discovered that before the 1914-18 war the room had been occupied by a very dissolute Russian grand duke, whose extravagancies had ruined the Russian consul, who had shot himself in this room.

In 1917 my grandfather's time in Ceylon ended and the family returned to England through submarine infested waters. Their convoy was attacked and they had to prepare to take to the lifeboats. One ship was sunk but their ship escaped, and they arrived in London to Zeppelin raids and Spanish 'flu. In 1918 my mother and father met again by chance on a Sussex railway station and soon became engaged at Liverpool, where daddy's ship was refitting.

3

Childhood

My parents were married on 1 January 1919 at Radlett in Hertfordshire. They then looked around for a house. They moved into The Elms in Maids Moreton, two miles from Buckingham on land belonging to Lady Kinloss, the heiress of the 3rd Duke of Buckingham and Chandos. Here Sheila and I were born by lamplight. English villages at this time, in the early twenties were completely rural. In the village there was a blacksmith; a communal bake-house, where the villagers brought their Sunday joints to be roasted; the rector had glebe land, where he grew fruit and vegetables and raised livestock, which was continually poached by his flock, as they knew when he would be in church, the squire, the farmers, and the farm labourers, as well as the doctor, who was locally nicknamed 'Pills'.

During the five years we spent at Maids Moreton, daddy was frequently away including a nine-month cruise around South America and at the Staff College at Greenwich. Though a lovely district, Buckingham in the centre of England, was hardly the most convenient place for a naval officer without a car. At this time they were rare and expensive. In fact, my father had taught himself to drive. A kind and trusting cousin of my mother's had lent them his Daimler to drive to Harrogate. Daddy had never driven before, but for the start of the journey they went with the cousin, Lindsay Fisher. Daddy amused him by always referring to left and right as port and starboard! However, they reached their destination without incident, thanks perhaps, to the scarcity of traffic at that time.

It was while we were at Maids Moreton that Lady Kinloss sold Stowe, which became the famous Public School, and whose grounds now belong to the National Trust. Lady Kinloss moved into the Dower House and became our immediate neighbour. Before she sold Stowe my mother and grandmother called on her there. They drove up in a hansom cab and rang the bell. To their surprise it was opened by Lady Kinloss herself, who explained that the servants never heard the bell, as the distances in the house were so great. Her grandfather, the 2nd Duke of Buckingham, had spent much of his vast fortune on furnishing Stowe. Indeed, when Queen Victoria and Prince Albert stayed there, the Queen remarked to Prince Albert, when she entered the bedroom assigned to them, 'Do you remember, Albert, this is the carpet we couldn't afford!' The duke had also lined the two-mile drive with his estate workers dressed in medieval costume to greet the royal couple. Though much impoverished by this expenditure, hence the sale of Stowe, Lady Kinloss still possessed priceless jewellery inherited from her Chandos ancestors. These she wore only once a year at the Buckingham Hunt Ball. One year she asked my father to accompany her in her car. (My mother could not go as she was expecting me.) Lady Kinloss was a magnificent sight on these occasions. She wore a simple dress of dark velvet, usually deep blue, to show off the diamonds. These consisted of a tiara, a stomacher, as well as a cross belt, entirely of diamonds, and other jewels. She was a small old lady and at the ball, everyone just said, 'Have you seen the diamonds?' My father was very relieved to reach the venue of the ball, as Lady Kinloss insisted on having all the lights in the car lit up. Luckily no thieves were around. Lady Kinloss said her dear father had told her always to bring the jewels from the bank in London, wrapped in brown paper and to sit in a third class carriage with her feet on the parcel. However, she seemed to have forgotten these excellent security measures, when she drove through the lonely Buckinghamshire countryside, the jewels illuminated by inside car lights!

Lady Kinloss's father had been a most enlightened Governor of Madras and had energetically grappled with the great famine there in 1867/8 and his daughter, Lady Kinloss (the only title she could inherit), was awarded the Crown of India for her work at that time. When the village mothers of Maids Moreton objected to having their children inoculated against smallpox, she went around to every house and cottage graphically describing, from personal experience, what an outbreak of smallpox was really like. The doctor had a queue for vaccinations next day!

My sister, Sheila a pretty fair-haired small girl, was a great favourite of Lady Kinloss, and after she came to live next door to us, was always running in and out of her garden and being given lilies and other flowers. Sheila, even at this early age seems to have foreseen her future diplomatic career. One day a kind, but very plain elderly lady came to call. She said to Sheila, much to my mother and grandmother's horror (granny was staying with us at the time), 'you know, when I was younger, someone said to me that I looked just like a monkey!' As she did look just like a monkey, it was with trepidation that they awaited the three-year old's reply. But Sheila answered with 'how unkind, and how untrue.'

Both Sheila had, and I have, very long and good memories. Sheila remembered my christening in Maids Moreton Church, when she was only two, and I can recall falling down the stairs at The Elms when I was one. I can also remember before I was two, being taken for a walk in my pram, while Sheila walked beside us, on a rainy day and thinking, 'Poor Sheila she will get so wet!' Not perhaps memorable moments, but my memory is coming in useful now, as it did for both of us in our different jobs in later years.

Our country life ended when father was appointed to the Malta dockyard in 1924. We lived in a tall old house in the capital, Valletta, facing Tigne harbour. Valletta was almost obliterated in the Second World War, but has now been reconstructed stone by stone. Malta was paradise for children; for as well as daily swimming in the Services' Club on the other side of the bay during the long summer months there were also frequent picnic parties. We usually went by motorboat. All of us children could swim, often better than our parents. We would jump from the highest rocks, holding our noses. I could swim in the harbour by the time I was three and one little boy was only eighteen months old. In fact he won a race, but was too small to understand that he must touch the post to win. When the fleet was in, there were marvellous ships' parties. The sailors dressed as pirates, helped us to slide down enormous chutes. At one party I spent the entire afternoon going up and down one chute, accompanied by my pirate, saying, 'more, more!' Sheila meanwhile, evidently at that age impervious to electric shocks, scooped money from containers with coins, the water of which had been lightly electrified. Eventually she was encouraged to move from this lucrative game. Meanwhile balloons were fired (or blown) from the 16" guns.

Malta was and is, full of historic sites and during these two years and on our next stay from 1927 to 1929, Sheila and I began our love affair with history. The island was occupied in turn by many great powers, as it holds the key to the Mediterranean. Both Napoleon and Nelson were here. The Grand Master of the Knights of St. John of Jerusalem took refuge in Malta after Rhodes fell to Islam in 1523. The Order's grandest hour was when, at immense sacrifice, the Knights resisted an enormous invasion by Süleyman I, the Magnificent in 1565.

The Grand Harbour, Malta

They then rebuilt their shattered fortresses and, in turn each Grand Master built vast churches even in the smallest villages, to the glory of God and perhaps, to remind the Maltese of their overlordship. The Maltese are among the most devout Roman Catholic Christians in the world. Feast days to honour all their particular saints, accompanied by clanging bells, carnivals, and fireworks were then and still are key points in their year. Of course at that time nobody could guess, that these courageous people would face a second siege as terrible as the first, against Hitler's *Luftwaffe* and the Italian navy. For their courage the island was awarded the George Cross and it was in the Grand Harbour that Admiral Cunningham received the surrender of the Italian fleet. This event however, was many years away. Though Sheila and I were only about six and eight, on this our second visit to the island, our governess Berry took us to every possible historic site and enthralled us with the stories of the Knights of Malta and the archaeological remains.

The halcyon years at Malta passed and my father was appointed to Portsmouth. We lived in a Queen Anne house in the old High Street, since demolished by bombs in World War II. It was beautiful downstairs but the attics, where Sheila and I and the two maids slept, were drafty and damp. The house also boasted a ghost, though none of us saw it. At this point a young French Swiss governess Simone, arrived to teach Sheila and me French. On the night of her arrival my mother found her on her knees, looking under the bed for the *chauffage central*. There was none of course. However, she gamely put up with this discomfort and taught us to speak French in a fortnight. She was very attractive and coming back from a day trip to London she was mistakenly picked up by a somewhat drunken sailor. He asked if he could carry her case? She not understanding, readily accepted the offer as British courtesy. But on reaching our house trouble developed as he wanted to come in. Luckily my father arrived. Police were called and next day the unfortunate sailor appeared before a Magistrate's Court. My mother had to act as interpreter. The bluejacket was fined and admonished for thus behaving to a young and innocent visitor to our shores. His language had evidently so shocked the worthy JPs that it had to be written down and the paper passed around to save the words being pronounced aloud. Simone was amazed at the speed of British justice, especially when my father told her that the sailor would receive additional punishment from his captain.

Sheila and I went to a small school in Southsea, where all I remember is singing 'God bless the Prince of Wales', (the future Duke of Windsor), learning arithmetic, which seems to have been largely ignored by our governess in Malta, so neither Sheila or I were either good at it or liked it. Sheila, an extremely bright child, also had to learn to write properly, though she was nine by this time. In Malta she had always inveigled Berry our governess, to write her essays at her dictation. It was a method she readopted later in her career when she never learned to type, but always dictated to secretaries! We also played with Sheila's Dalmatian, Rex, on Southsea Common. He was extremely disobedient and one day leapt out of the car's sunroof on top of a lady cyclist. She was not amused and Rex had to be sold to a country owner much to our great sadness. On weekends we drove into the country and played games in the New Forest or on the Portsdown Hills, not then covered by commuter houses. I was also run over in Southsea by a small van and concussed. It went over my legs (I was seven) but the bicycle must have saved them being broken. I was carried home and recovered quite quickly.

In the early 1930s my father's time in the Navy was now temporarily ended. The 'Geddes Axe' caught him, when the Royal Navy was drastically cut due to the economic climate at that time. He rose above his disappointment at the seeming end of his naval career and only said that he expected a better man than he had been promoted. He did not know that in the Second World War he would be given the post of King's Harbour Master, which as a navigator, he had always longed for. Actually he immediately obtained a civilian job as Harbour Master in

Port Sudan on the Red Sea. Sheila and I were necessarily at that time, left in England.

4

Education and Travel in Continental Europe

Meanwhile Sheila, aged eleven and I, aged nine, were dispatched as boarders to a small private school, Herons Ghyll, on the outskirts of Horsham in Sussex. I was miserably homesick. This of course did not last too long. The school was an attractive building set in lovely gardens, which were bordered by fields. Luckily we both enjoyed lessons, especially as Herons Ghyll leaned heavily towards the humanities: English, history, religious instruction and French. Biology was not taught at all as I suspect, that Miss Brown and Miss Neave, the joint headmistresses, thought that sex might appear on the curriculum. Botany was allowed though, as I could not draw I was very bad at it, and I suspect Sheila was even worse, so we did not like it. But what I enjoyed most at school were the games. Luckily I had a good eye and captained the tennis team to victory against the other private schools of West Sussex. Team games bored Sheila and she would, as often as possible kindly volunteer to take girls back to school if they were hit at lacrosse, a somewhat violent game. She would then curl up by the fire and read a book!

In the two years our parents were abroad - though my mother came back in the summer - we were farmed out on friends and relations during the holidays. The first Christmas was not too sad as we stayed with our devoted grandparents. They spoiled us nicely and employed an elderly lady to take us sightseeing. After being inveigled into climbing to the Cross on the dome of St Paul's, she resigned!

On her way home from the Sudan to spend the summer holidays with Sheila and me, my mother was on the deck of her ship, which was approaching Marseilles. She realized that granddaddy was standing beside her and a few minutes later a steward came up to her with a signal saying that he had suddenly died from a heart attack in London. Mummy and my grandfather had always been exceptionally close.

One of the best things at Herons Ghyll were the summer Shakespeare play. All the school took part and in this way we got to know almost the entire plays we were acting by heart, even if we only had minor parts. It also trained us in public speaking, especially as we acted in the garden, so it was necessary to speak audibly. The producer was the much feared Miss Brown, who had trained at a dramatic school. I think the plays attained a good amateur standing and performances were always crowded with friends and parents. Proceeds went to the Chailey Home for Disabled Children near Lewes. During my last years the stage was floodlit. Sussex has probably the best weather in the United Kingdom and I only remember one performance being rained out. Our first year, when I was nine and Sheila eleven, we took part in *Julius Caesar*, and though we were only rather small members of Mark Antony's crowd, I can still recall practically every speech. This knowledge of many of Shakespeare's plays stood me in good stead for subsequent exams, even, after the war at university.

Most of the plays went off very well, but there was one disastrous *Henry IV*, in any case a very unsuitable play for girls. Horses had been hired to add authenticity and liveliness to the performance. Well it added liveliness. The girl who took the part of Henry IV was an indifferent rider and when she mounted her steed, he was so put off by her fake armour that he bolted down the front drive, as all the parents were arriving in their cars. He galloped out into the lane pursued by the foxhunting 'Prince Hal'. Poor King Henry was thrown at a brook in St Leonard's Forest. Bandaged, but undaunted, she eventually rode on to the lawn proclaiming the aptly suitable first lines - "So shaken as we are, so wan with care" there was great applause, but there were more mishaps to follow. One bucolic scene had been arranged round a maypole. We small ones had all rehearsed the intricate steps for weeks, but alas, some unfortunate girl danced her rope the wrong way round and we ended in a tight knot, only to be disentangled by the humiliated Miss Brown. Later in the doomed play, Sheila a slight fourteen-year old, had been surprisingly cast as the Welsh warrior, Owen Glendower. At one stage she called for her ally to 'sit, fair cousin,' and there was no chair!

Henry IV was the exception and I remember an excellent *Winter's Tale*, when Sheila was an outstanding Paulina. The play is full of sexual allusions. Miss Brown and Miss Neave had spent much of their Easter holidays blacking out some of the most lurid passages in the cast copies. Not a good idea, as plays of Shakespeare are easy to find and we all looked up the forbidden passages, which, probably, in that innocent age, we would not have otherwise understood.

The most memorable performance, from my point of view, was when I played Prospero in *The Tempest*. I was given the part during the Christmas term of 1937. The play was the set book for the School Certificate (the equivalent of GCSE), which my form was taking. I began to learn some of the very long early speeches when I became ill. I had had violent stomach attacks all through the summer holidays. They lasted for some hours, and then stopped completely. But during this last bout the local GP happened to be in the school and diagnosed gallstones, though this condition was almost unknown in a thin fifteen-year old. Subsequent X-rays proved him right and I had my gall bladder removed at University College Hospital. I was not able to return to Herons Ghyll until April. At Christmas Miss Brown, I thought most unfairly, wrote to say she had assigned Prospero to a girl called Adrienne and I was given the dull part of a lord. However, fate was on my side. The night before the dress rehearsal, Adrienne came down with German measles and Miss Brown had to beg me to take on Prospero. I abandoned all lessons and learned the part in twenty-four hours, improvising slightly as I went along. Rosemary Ogilvie, who was playing Miranda my stage daughter, is still my best friend. She kept offering me the magic cloak when I least expected it. By the first night I really did know the words and much enjoyed the occasion, though I had nightmares for several years that I was on a stage without knowing my part.

Sheila and I had gone to Herons Ghyll on the advice of Olive Archer, my mother's best friend, whom she had met on their adventurous voyage back from Ceylon in 1917. Olive all her life was very beautiful and at twenty had married a much older man, already the Governor of Uganda. From there he had been summoned to take over the Governor-Generalship of the Sudan on the murder of the previous Governor-General, Sir Lee Stack, in Cairo. There were no roads and I think Olive was carried through the jungle on a palanquin as she and Sir Geoffrey hurried north. He was a giant of a man - 6ft. 7 inches tall-and with his lovely young wife won the admiration of the warlike Sudanese but also the jealousy of the High Commissioner for Egypt and the Sudan, a much cleverer man, but in physique much smaller so not so impressive to the locals. This latent antagonism between the two men was not helped when Lord Lloyd came on an official visit to Khartoum. He was Sir Geoffrey's immediate superior. Some weeks before the Queen Dowager, Queen Alexandra, had died. Khartoum went into court mourning until after the funeral, but then reverted to normal dress. The Sudan was in the middle of the hot weather season. All the ladies had prepared their best dresses for the Governor's garden party. Olive wore a particularly attractive one in brilliant colours which she later gave my mother. The state train arrived at Khartoum station and all the officials including the Archers, were drawn up to meet them. The train stopped and Lady Lloyd emerged dressed from head to foot in black, her face veiled by black lace. Olive went up to greet her and apologised for her lack of mourning, explaining that due to the heat, they had shortened the requisite official mourning. Lady Lloyd replied icily, and with a break in her voice, 'Of course, I was a lady-in-waiting to the dear Queen...' All the ladies coming to the garden party had to be warned, and tailors throughout Khartoum spent all night sewing up black clothes.

Olive became Sheila's godmother and her sister Hester, who had married (Col.) Jack Colvin, and their cousin Di Thursby, my two godmothers. We spent a great deal of time at their father, old Colonel Godman's house, Woldringfold. Before my mother and father went out to Port Sudan we stayed there for six months, when Sheila and I first went to Herons Ghyll. Colonel Godman was the sixth and youngest son of his father, a rich industrialist, who had set up all his children in magnificent houses that they built or bought, across England. The widow of the eldest son, the remarkable, but very kind Dame Alice, and their two daughters Eva and Edith, owned Woldringfold's neighbouring estate, South Lodge. Woldringfold was built of Sussex stone with high chimneys and had a wonderful view over the Weald of Sussex to the distant South Downs. Inside there was a square hall with a huge inglenook fireplace (a fireplace within the sitting area). Growling lion and tiger heads adorned the walls, shot I think, by Sir Geoffrey. One day daddy amused everyone by putting apples between their teeth. Gardens and a ha-ha (a sunk fence) surrounded the house.

Colonel Godman, then in his eighties was a fine old man and took a great liking to my father. His chauffeur was his other favourite. I remember his telling me how as a boy, he had been looking towards Chichester when at that moment the great spire of the cathedral collapsed inwards. (It was later rebuilt). He still had the stagecoach in a garage, which he had driven annually between London and Brighton. I suppose he remembered when the railways displaced these coaches. By the time we went to school Olive had come to keep house for her father, as her marriage had broken up.

South Lodge (an extraordinary name for such a huge house, now a hotel) was not as attractive a building as Woldringfold, but the gardens were a delight to horticulturalists, full of exotic trees, shrubs and flowers. Dame Alice was kindness itself to us and once lent the house to mummy and daddy for a week while she was away. It was still staffed by a solemn butler, called Petley, two footmen, and innumerable other servants. Before she left Dame Alice told my father 'My dear husband said to me "Alice, should the house catch fire, please rescue me first, then the china"' (They owned priceless Persian pottery). Daddy wondered if in such a situation he ought to give priority to the china rather than to my mother!

While mummy and daddy were luxuriating at South Lodge, Sheila and I went with Eva and Edith, (both County Commissioners) to a guide camp on the South Downs. We hated it, as we had to sleep on mattresses filled with hay which were alive with earwigs. In the evenings we sat round a campfire and sang jolly songs. As neither Sheila, the Godman sisters nor I could sing, this was far from jolly! On the last Saturday the other guides' parents were brought down to see their offspring and to have a day at the sea. Sheila was left in the camp to prepare tea for about thirty people. I wondered how she would cope. I need not have worried. When we got back from the beach all the sandwiches were superbly cut and everything prepared. Petley had stopped off on the way and taken over, while Sheila just did the flowers!

Sheila and my school terms were interrupted when Sheila was diagnosed with suspected heart trouble after measles in 1934. By this time father's job in the Sudan had ended and he was fully retired. Sheila's specialist obligingly suggested that a spell in the Alps would reinvigorate her and as mummy and daddy were much run down after the formidable heat of the Sudan - no air-conditioning then - we all set off for the Tyrol. At that time Sterling was very good value against the Austrian schilling. As our parents were fairly hard-up they decided that we should stay part of the next few years at a small pension, called the Jagerhof, at Schoenberg, in the Stubaital. It was delightful. Quite small, it contained about twenty rooms, all spotlessly clean, with the forerunners of duvets on the beds and beautiful views over the mountains which bordered Italy. A family called Auer ran it. They had originated in the South Tyrol but had moved north, when the Treaty of Versailles handed over that province to Italy. Frau Auer was an excellent cook, her son ran the hotel, and their daughter, Gisella, waited at tables. We became almost part of the family and when we came back from visits to England, or other travels, we were always greeted in our bedroom by a huge chocolate cake. Schoenberg was a lovely village. (Sadly it has now been completely spoiled by the *autobahn*, which has chopped the village in half). It lies 3,000 ft. above sea level and the meadows, which surround it, are covered with wild flowers in the spring and summer and snow in the winter. Indeed it snowed the night we came in November 1934, and I will never forget the glare from the snow on the first morning, for we had arrived when it was already dark.

Fulpmes, Tyrol, Austria

The first year we did not have a car, but the next year daddy bought a small but tough Standard, and we drove everywhere. In the spring and summer holidays we set off for Italy, Prague, or Vienna, staying at small hotels and sightseeing. Daddy got used to driving in the snow during the winter and we often went across the border to Munich or to watch the run-up to the Olympic Winter games at Seefeld.

That first year we were lucky enough to have made friends with a very attractive Hungarian, Dinko de Balla. He came from an old Hungarian family, which had been temporarily ruined after the First World War. Dinko had escaped from the Central European chaos to take a ship to

America, working as a deck hand. Unfortunately, his elite education had prepared him for duelling, not fisticuffs, and, until he learned to defend himself from his rough shipmates he had a difficult time. Arriving penniless in the USA, he took a job in a factory, where his wages only paid for his board and lodging. He was a virtual slave. He escaped one night and somehow made his way to a city in Maryland, where he obtained an academic post and met his future wife a charming American, Kitty. When he first came to the Jagerhof he was still unmarried and fell in love, in a somewhat mystical way, with Sheila (then 15) whom he tried, unsuccessfully, to convert to Catholicism. Towards the end of the first winter he returned to America, married Kitty and brought her to Austria on their honeymoon, just before Easter 1935. He then suggested he should drive the four of us with them to Budapest, where his mother and brother Boris, were living. We wondered if his bride would mind, but as an American, and not speaking any language but English, I think she was delighted. The friendship survived and in later years during the war, she invited mummy, Sheila, and me to take refuge with her family in Maryland, after daddy had been killed in 1943. Though grateful, we did not, of course accept.

In Budapest Dinko insisted, I think rightly, that we should stay at the best hotel despite its high price. At this period we had little spare money, but he said we could eat out even at breakfast, and that would give us a much better impression of the city from a first class hotel. Admiral Horthy was in power. We met one of his ministers and his family talking in German. The Admiral had commanded gunboats in the First World War and the minister was fascinated that my father had served in them in Mesopotamia. We were also taken to a very long Palm Sunday service in a village church outside Budapest, where all the peasants were dressed in their traditional colourful costumes. The Long Gospel was read in turn in Latin, Magyar and Serb, none of which we could understand. Daddy made my youth, I was only twelve, an excuse for taking me out at this point, but mother and Sheila stoically endured the two-hour service, while daddy and I took photos. In the afternoon, Dinko suggested that mummy and Sheila should accompany him and Kitty to hear a famous preacher speaking in Magyar, in a slum church in Pest. Meanwhile daddy and I were taken to a gourmet café and partook of wonderful cakes! Evidently the church was crammed with none-too clean peasantry and there were no seats. My mother then fainted and so the expedition was rapidly terminated.

In the evening the rest of the family was taken to a famous fish restaurant on an island in the Danube for dinner. (I was too young to go). Poor mother choked on a fishbone and was in agony until she saw a doctor next day, who told her that the bone had cut either side of her throat and she might have died. There had been a strange prelude to this accident. A month before when we were walking in the Tyrolean mountains with our Austrian *Fraulein*, my mother noticed a wayside shrine. 'Who is that saint?' she asked, 'and what is he revered for?' *Fraulein* answered, 'That is St. Blaise, the patron saint for those suffering from swallowing fishbones.' My mother I am sorry to say, laughed and replied, 'He can't have much to do!' She remembered St. Blaise in Budapest and never made fun of him again!

We always during the four years we spent on the Continent, came home to England for part of the spring and summer and Sheila and I returned to Herons Ghyll, though Sheila for only one term, to take her School Certificate.

Many of these summers, and before, when we were living in Portsmouth, we visited our Harden cousins at Harrybrook. Harrybrook was and still is though no longer belonging to the family a large, rambling Georgian house in Co. Armagh, Northern Ireland. The cousins, who were some years older than Sheila and me - Esmé, Toby, Molly and the long-awaited son Dick, became lifelong friends, as have their children. When we first arrived there, they were rather alarmed at the thought of starchy English relations.

The three girls decided it would be ladylike to be doing the flowers when we arrived. But they spoiled the effect by jumping out of the windows to greet us. We immediately clicked and had many happy holidays there. We swam in the cold river and played 'murder' in the evenings, creeping through the house searching for victims. We often went to watch the Tourist Trophy driving race which at that time, took place through country villages, cleared for the event, but still very dangerous as they then used ordinary cars not the robot-like machines you see now. There was always a family sweepstake and on the way home, all the male drivers behaved as if they were taking part in the TT! On such occasions the house was so full that some of the guests had to sleep in the baths!

The first year we went to Harrybrook, Esmé became engaged to a delightful young clergyman, Dickie King, the son of the Dean of Derry, when we were all on a picnic in the Mourne Mountains. He later became Chaplain to the Forces and then rector of Almer. He was much loved, but sadly died young.

The next sister Toby was engaged to a handsome young doctor, Jock Lord. Their wedding took place the next year in Clare church. Sheila was a bridesmaid and later became godmother to their daughter Elizabeth, and more recently, to her daughter Harriet. The wedding was enormous fun, despite the predictable Irish wet weather and the naughty little pages.

Harrybrook in County Armagh is situated in, what in recent years has become, one of the most troubled parts of the province. Naturally as I was still a child, I was not much aware of the religious climate. I remember though that when the youngest, and yet unmarried sister, Molly founded a village hockey team, it was a surprise that she included both Protestant and Catholic youths in her team. There was a match with this team against the house party. It was quite difficult to find enough players in the house. Sheila and I, aged 10 and 12, were enlisted, though we had never played hockey, and so was my mother, who somewhat unfairly was placed in goal to face the enormous Irish youths. Daddy, Jock, Toby, and Dick could all play quite well and Molly had to be on our side, though she was umpire and obviously rooting for her local team. Luckily the game was a draw, but acrimony against Molly lasted all evening, as the family accused her of bias in her umpiring!

To return to the problem of discrimination, this certainly did take place, for Toby told me later that no Catholics were allowed to work on the estate and the family only patronized Protestant run shops. We were over once on the 12th of July, Lundy Day - he had opened the gates of Derry to King James - and though some of his effigy burning was comic (they used Jim's top hat each year, rescuing it at the last minute) there was a latent unpleasantness about the proceedings. After Toby married and moved with Jock, who had a practice, first at Burnley then at Longridge in Lancashire, her father Jim, warned her never to go to a Catholic owned shop. Naturally she ignored this advice and their best friends were Catholics and later in life Jock was chosen as doctor to Stonyhurst a large and very beautiful Catholic public school near Longridge outside Preston, where he was hugely popular. Dick after the war, became MP for Armagh and treated all his constituents equally. He laughed and told me once that at his election the cry had been, 'Up with King William, and down with King James!' Jim too a local JP, was absolutely fair in his judgments, and once told us with a smile, how an elderly woman had been had up for swearing about the Pope. 'What have you against him, my good woman?' asked Jim. She answered! 'He hasn't got a good name in Portadown!'

Sheila left Herons Ghyll in 1935 and went to a charming aristocratic German family in Munich, the Podevils - a Count and Countess. They came from Bohemia and were extremely anti-Nazi. Indeed, the Gräfin at a good deal of risk to herself and family, not only rescued her elderly old Jewish governess from Dachau, but arranged for her to teach the English girls including Sheila, she had taken to learn German, and to help with the von Podevils depleted income. This governess told Sheila that she remembered seeing the handsome, but mad Bavarian king, Ludwig II, ride past her on a snowy night in his sleigh. He never liked to be seen and so always escaped to the mountains as often as possible. Here he built his Wagnerian castles: Neuerschwanstein, Linderhof, and Chiemsee. At that time they were considered enormous tax consumers, though Ludwig always remained extremely popular, but by now these castles must have more than paid for their building, not only for their strange, fantastic beauty, but also for the tourist trade they have engendered.

The Nazis had a strong following in Austria before the *Anschluss*. I think mainly because the Austrians had been so humiliated by the terms of the Treaty of Versailles, when the great Empire of the Hapsburgs had been carved up. Every year in January or February, one would wake to see huge swastikas painted by Nazi skiers on the precipitous slopes of the Nordkette, the line of mountains that divided Innsbruck and the Inn Valley from Bavaria. We travelled in and through Germany often during the years from 1934, (when Dollfuss was murdered in Vienna,) to 1938.

There were Nazi flags everywhere, soldiers marching through the streets singing the Horst Wessel song etc., but as Anglo-Saxons we were always treated in a friendly and helpful way. The only sinister marks of Hitler's regime were anti-Jewish signs on shop windows in Germany. I cannot remember any in pre-*Anschluss* Austria. However, we were aware of Nazi remilitarisation by talking to the British Consul General in Munich, Donald Gainer, (later Sir Donald) who often stayed at the Jagerhof. He spoke perfect German and constantly warned the Foreign Office of the covert rearming of Germany. He always attended the Nuremberg rallies and told us what charismatic powers of oratory Hitler possessed. Even he who loathed every aspect of Nazism, had difficulty restraining himself from joining the thunderous applause that greeted the Fuhrer's every sentence. Sadly Sir Donald's telegrams went largely unheeded. Lady Gainer told me that she had seen boys as young as ten or eleven instructed in hand grenade throwing.

Innsbruck and the Nordkette

However, war was still some years away and Sheila much enjoyed her six months with the Graf and Gräfin. They had two older children, but their youngest nicknamed Bubi, was Sheila's age, sixteen. They were good friends and Sheila went on many expeditions to the mountains of Bavaria, to dances with the young officer cadets, and to historic sites with the Gräfin. She also taught them etiquette, probably even then, an old-fashioned type. For instance, when a member of the ex-Bavarian royalty came on a visit it was necessary for the whole household to be at the door to greet them. Very naturally Sheila and Bunty the other English girl, had stayed in the background feeling they might be in the way, but this was not correct. At this time the provincial allegiances were still very marked. For instance, the Graf's eldest daughter Madie - also a Gräfin, hence the proliferation of a noble class, unlike Great Britain with its rules of primogeniture - always signed a register abroad with her nationality as Bavarian.

It was at the recommendation of the Gräfin that Sheila went to the family in Paris, with Madame Marie-Louise Marquet, a widow to study

French. Here Sheila spent eighteen months and towards the end became so bilingual that Marie-Louise suggested to my mother that she should enrol at the Sorbonne for the degré supérieur in French Civilization. Sheila took four subjects: French history, Art, Literature and Philosophy. The exams, all both written and oral, conducted entirely in French, were very stiff and Sheila was one of only 19 out of 189 who received a degree.

Sheila loved her time in Paris and Marie-Louise took her and the one or two other boys and girls of varying nationalities around all the sights, to the opera and plays, and also to their country cottage (she shared it with a friend), near Compiègne. One English boy Adrian and Sheila became great friends. One day they thought it would be fun to attend a séance. They found out where it was to be held and joined the very solemn and credulous audience. The medium began telling them that she saw an aura round somebody's head. Adrian and Sheila were now so convulsed with laughter that they had to be expelled from the meeting. By this time, I imagine they had completely broken the atmosphere! It was while Sheila was in France that Germany had occupied the Rhineland. Germany had already taken back the industrial areas to the east the year before. This time it was touch and go whether France would retaliate, but in 1936 neither side was ready and the situation was diffused.

Meanwhile, I always managed to spend the Easter term skiing with my parents and naturally, became fairly proficient. In those days there were very few ski lifts. The only one near us was up the Patscherkofl, a mountain the other side of the valley leading up to the Brenner Pass. Some distant cousins came to spend the first Christmas we were at the Jagerhof in Igls, below this mountain. The four of us went over one day with Fortune Smith, a friend of Sheila's. Six of us daddy, Charles Cooper, his nephew, John, Fortune, Sheila and I decided to ski down. It was a difficult and steep run and none of us had skied for more than a week or two. We left the remainder of the party at the top of the cable railway and set off, while the others went down in the ski lift. Six hours later we had not reappeared. The experts did this descent in ten minutes! However, we had never been in any danger but Sheila lost a ski temporarily, and she and Fortune spent most of those hours on their backsides. The home party thought we were all dead!

Many friends from England over the next four years, came out and joined us. Admiral Brodie (Brodles) a naval friend of the family came many times, both summer and winter. (His wife, Lucy, did not come because she was lame.) Brodles a natural athlete, only took up skiing in his fifties, but threw himself down the mountains with extraordinary bravado. Strangely enough he never hurt himself skiing but broke two ribs in the summer, trying to shut a skylight in our bathroom! Once Herr Auer the hotel manager had to write to his wife and much amused her by addressing his envelope to Mrs Brodie, Admiral's Mate. I think he thought this a particularly appropriate naval title!

A lovely two-day expedition was to the Maria Waldrast monastery. We drove up to Matrei, near the Brenner, then shouldered our skis and climbed up the steep path, bordering a mountain stream, to the monastery. This path had the Stations of the Cross in small shrines all the way up. There were fourteen and it seemed a long, long way. We usually stayed the night at the monastery, sleeping in male or female dormitories. These had a good fire burning in a huge stove, when we went to bed, but in the morning it was freezing and we shivered under the duvets. Eventually the bravest, usually mummy, got up and lit the logs. I was often left alone in the evening as I was usually much the youngest of the party, and was alarmed if I ventured into the long corridors, which were very dimly lit. At one end I remember, there was a sombre painting of a huge monk, which made it spookier. In the morning, after breakfast, we donned skins over our skis. Actually ours were made of some sort of material, which was cheaper than fur, and climbed the last thousand feet to the summit. After that it was pure heaven. One skied on unbroken powder snow for the two thousand feet of fairly gentle descents through woods and across meadows back to Schoenberg. I never remember ever meeting other skiers. Sometimes one saw passing woodsmen guiding their laden sleighs down the hillside, which they cleverly manoeuvred down the steep and icy paths with their feet. We never took a guide, as there was no fear of avalanches on these slopes. Daddy had bought a ciné camera and he would position himself at the bottom of a difficult run and take pictures of us all skiing down. It was amusing afterwards to see how people began to lose their balance quite early on and then quite gradually descended into a snowy heap at the bottom of the slope. There were very few accidents. I think probably, because the uphill climbing toughened our muscles and other skiers did not get in our way.

A number of girls of Sheila's age came out and joined us at various times, as well as a friend from Herons Ghyll, Margaret Lampson and her elder brother Graham. In 1937 their father, Sir Miles Lampson, (later Lord Killearn) had just been appointed to Cairo as British Ambassador, and they came to Schoenberg for Christmas. We all had tremendous fun and our varying ages seemed to have made no difference. Sometimes we climbed up to the huts which are still scattered over the Alps. Some were very basic, with bi-sexual dormitories and minimal washing arrangements; others like the Stephanshütte, on the Stubai glacier had separate tiny rooms. Food was always provided, at least where we stayed, but it sometimes ran out and once we ate *Apfelstrudel* for breakfast. The Stephanshütte took six hours to reach. I climbed it with daddy and Brodles my last year and it was the only time I skied over a glacier. It was quite dangerous and while we were walking up an avalanche came down through the middle of our separated party. Luckily it missed us all.

In the summer, when we were not in England with friends or Ireland at Harrybrook and, in the Easter holidays, (I did return to school at Herons Ghyll sometimes), we took off in our little Standard to explore Western Europe. Once we drove to Berlin, via Prague. It happened to be May Day and the city was filled with Nazi parades and banners. One summer we drove as far south as Sorrento, stopping at many of the great and beautiful Italian cities on the way. I have since revisited most of them and it is sad to see how so many new buildings encase the old towns, though the Italians have been clever in making many of their centres pedestrianized.

My mother did have a strange experience in Perugia. We knew nothing about the town, but we discovered an old inn down a side street backing on the ancient walls. Mummy, in her faltering Italian, asked for a room and the hotelier showed her rather an unattractive one, with no view. ((Sheila and I were on the floor above.) 'Is there nothing better?' asked my mother. 'Yes there is this one', he answered reluctantly, and showed us a lovely bedroom with a fantastic view over the Umbrian countryside. 'Of course I had rather have this,' she said. We spent a carefree evening playing rummy and then Sheila and I went up to bed. My mother woke suddenly at five to twelve and there was a most horrible atmosphere in the room. She felt compelled to get out of bed and go to the window. She looked down at the new town, where they were playing modern music, but she knew that made no difference. She forced herself to go back again towards her bed, but again she felt impelled to move towards the window. Suddenly a clock struck midnight and all the evil departed. She woke my father and next morning we moved on. It was not until about twenty-five years later that we had a possible explanation of this happening. Our friends the Rubinsteins, who were specialists in the Italian Renaissance, were dining with us. Mummy happened to mention that she had bad memories of Perugia and told them of this occurrence. 'How extraordinary,' said Ruth 'because Perugia's greatest soldier at this time, Braccio Montone, was chronicled by Pope Pius II Piccolomini, not only for his horrific cruelty, unusual even at this time, also for throwing his enemies from the ramparts.

As I have already described, the *Anschluss* came quite suddenly and we were advised by the British consul in Innsbruck to leave Austria immediately. We drove back to the Jagerhof, packed our cases, just leaving our ski things with Herr Auer. (Alas, we never returned till after the war, but before that he had returned everything back to England in 1946.) The BBC news was very melodramatic and announced that German troops were massing on the Brenner. In the event it was quite quiet and we drove down to the Italian lakes and then on to Florence. This was a peaceful interlude before war came. I have never known Florence to be more beautiful. It was Easter time and the sun was already hot. The streets and piazzas were relatively free from tourists, due I suppose to the deteriorating political situation. We stayed in a charming old pensione called the San Giorgio, by the Pitti Palace, sadly to receive a direct hit in 1944. From Florence we drove slowly through France back to England. In London at his club 'the Senior', (the United Services Club) daddy came across a naval acquaintance he had met a few weeks earlier at the Innsbruck consulate. He had had a much more difficult return to England. His train had been stopped at the border. It was filled with fleeing Jews and though they were allowed to continue their journeys, all their possessions were seized and the carriage seats were ripped open to see if they were concealing money. Also before he left, his Austrian friend with whom he had been staying, tried to shoot himself.

As soon as we reached England my father was recalled to the Navy and appointed Boom Defence Officer, Ceylon. This was May 1938. The lion was slowly flexing its paws and rearming had begun. Daddy was delighted. At last he had work again and was sent to Rosyth for training. Meanwhile, Sheila was 'coming out'. A friend lent us a little house behind Harrods. Sheila had a lovely summer, being presented at Court and then going to a Royal Garden Party. It was necessary for someone, who had themselves been presented to the King, to present their daughter, or daughters, or a friend's daughter. As my mother and grandmother had both been presented in their day this provided no problems, and Sheila had a lovely white dress made for her. Three feathers (in honour of the Princes of Wales) were set on her head and she was taught to curtsey by Madame Vacani. Sheila did the Season and went to many friends' dances and parties. As she was very pretty and attractive, she enjoyed it all very much. Indeed, one old colonel told me the other day how he had proposed to Sheila under a cherry tree that summer at the Sandhurst Ball. Throughout her life, Sheila had many proposals - once three in one day - but she never married.

Meanwhile I had returned to school, where I performed as Prospero, won various tennis tournaments and was confirmed. My confirmation took place in the lovely downland church at South Harting. The then Bishop of Lewes a saintly old man confirmed me. Both Sheila and I have been fortunate that our parents and grandparents were all deeply committed members of the Church of England. We also have many friends and relations who are Catholics and so Christianity and ecumenism has always been a most important and integral part of our lives.

5

Ceylon

It had been planned for me, like Sheila, to finish my education learning German and French. Indeed, in 1938 I had been entered as a pupil with a family of Bavarians, who lived near Garmisch-Partenkirchen in the Bavarian Alps. At this time I was madly addicted to skiing, and there I could carry on with this, while learning German. However, Hitler intervened. Mummy and daddy were sailing for Ceylon (now Sri Lanka) in October just after Chamberlain's famous meeting at Berchtesgaden. War was postponed but Sheila and I were not to be left behind and we too set out off for the East. When we learned the news we were so excited that we danced round the table at the house of cousins where we were staying! Then we rushed to the London shops buying outfits for a hot climate. Clothes have not really changed very much over all these years, we bought and subsequently wore trousers, shorts, shirts, evening dresses, and cotton frocks, very similar to those I wear today, except, perhaps for the evening dresses. But I still wear cotton housecoats, which we wore when we were at home in Ceylon and which I still wear every evening now. Dress in London, however, remained formal till World War II.

As Sheila and my departures were so last minute we had to travel in a different ship to mummy and daddy's P & O. Our ship was smaller and I suspect the captain had a penchant for drink. In any event he nearly ran us aground on a Red Sea island. Otherwise the journey was uneventful and our fellow passengers boring. Indeed, we were so fed up with their company that we were about to slip off the ship at Port Said and explore it on our own, certainly unwise for sixteen and eighteen year old girls, when we were summoned to the captain's cabin. Granny had put us in his charge, when we left London, but he had never spoken a word to us before. 'I hope you are going ashore with a nice large party?' he asked. We reluctantly admitted that we had decided to go on our own. He was horrified and we spent the afternoon and evening in the company of our shipmates. Actually some of them became rather drunk, while we watched the most pathetic floor show at one of the large hotels. Elderly artistes, so aged that they could hardly bend their knees, let alone engage in erotic dances, performed. It was indeed the end of the road for them.

We arrived in Ceylon in October 1938 to be met by our parents. Neither of us had ever been to the East before and I shall never forget the colour, the hubbub, and the excitement of arriving in Colombo. Everywhere I saw men spitting what I thought was blood on the road, only to find it was the juice of betel nut that they continually chewed! Friends appeared from nowhere and we were immediately swept up into tennis at the Garden Club, parties in the evenings, though at first I was considered too young for these, and excursions. We rented a flat opposite the Galle Face Hotel. The days seemed rather long, as it was too hot to go out until about 5 o'clock, then we would play tennis and Sheila played golf. One day I noticed in the local paper *The Times of Ceylon* that there was to be the Junior Tennis Championship of Ceylon for under eighteens. It was to be held at the Ceylonese Tennis Club, so I went there with my parents and enrolled. Considering that the Garden Club, the European Club, was not open to Ceylonese, it was very kind of everyone to have been so welcoming to me and remembered that I was granddaughter to Sir Alexander, who had been very popular in the island. This tournament made me first aware of colour prejudice. As no white girl had ever entered the championship before, my entry caused quite a stir and for the only time in my life I saw my name in headlines in the sports page of *The Times of Ceylon*. Miss Harden reaches semi-finals. Miss Harden in finals. Sadly I was beaten 7-5 in the final set, so only took the runners-up cup. Actually I could have played for another two years, as my opponent was older than me, but I expect a better player would have turned up. In any event, once again Hitler stepped in!

The girl who won was very attractively dressed in a blue sari, which must have been most encumbering, but she played with great skill and I remember one of the boys in their events was the first player who I ever recall, using two hands for a backhand shot. There were many good tennis players in Ceylon and later one of the adult male champions, Lt. Fonseca, served under my father in the Ceylonese navy in Trinco. He often made up a foursome with me, daddy, (a good player,) and some other man, but normally he never bothered to show his real skill, as it would have made a poor game. One day though a signal came for my father and he said he would have to go at the end of the game. Lt. Fonseca won in three shots!

Just before Christmas 1938, Admiral Sir James Somerville with Lady Somerville and their daughter, Rachel, arrived with the Eastern Fleet in Colombo. Sir James and daddy were old shipmates. Although much senior, he had served with daddy in Malta and Sheila and Rachel were great friends. Sheila went with them for a visit when the fleet moved to Trincomalee (always called Trinco), for a short stay, meeting a rogue elephant on the drive up. They lived in Admiralty House. This building had been built in the eighteenth century and all the rooms led out from the central dining room. Built I suppose by a naval inspired architect, on the instruction of some admiral, who wanted his shore establishment to look as much like a battleship as possible. It was hardly a sensible plan as in the days before air conditioning, the only hope of keeping cool was to let the evening breezes circulate. Also Sheila said the house was inhabited by the most enormous ants she had ever seen and who were particularly partial to her old fashioned bathroom.

Coast of Ceylon

Sir James as well as being extraordinarily kind and loved by all who served with him, was one of the most amusing raconteurs I have ever known. At huge dinner parties, which he often gave in his flagship, the whole company would stop talking to each other in order to listen to him. One story I particularly remember: when serving as a young officer based in the Mediterranean his ship had been presented with a brown bear by the Russians, when they were visiting the Black Sea. The bear was very popular with the ship's company and became a great pet and their mascot. However, when it was hot, it liked a swim. One day in Malta Harbour it went for a bathe. Unfortunately while it was swimming, its ship's gangway had been drawn up. The bear looked around and seeing another one lowered, it approached and climbed up it. In fact this had been prepared for the official visit of the Spanish consul. To his horror he saw the bear and wisely decided to give it precedence. Thus the officers manning the top of the gangway found themselves saluting a brown bear! The subsequent signal to the offending ship was not repeatable and the bear's mascot days came to an abrupt end.

At that time girls did not 'come out' until they were seventeen or eighteen and when Sir James invited us all to a Christmas ball on board his flagship my mother thought I was too young to go. I was sixteen. 'Nonsense,' Sir James laughingly replied, 'half my midshipmen are about her age.' It was my first grown-up dance and it was magical. The ship was brilliantly lit and decorated and Sir James kept coming up to see that my programme was filled. I wore a shimmery white dress and he called me The White Lady.

During this pre-war period we had a flat opposite the Galle Face Hotel, but spent several weeks in the naval base in Trinco, staying at the Welcome Hotel - the only one there at that time. As my father's job, until the war was supervising the building of the boom defences at both Trinco and Colombo, he spent a great deal of time in Trinco, usually staying with the Swindells the civilian head of the dockyard.

It was during one of our visits to Trinco that I had my first and truly dreadful introduction to sailing. Like all naval officers my father was a perfectly proficient small boat sailor, but he much preferred spending the short evening light playing tennis. One day he came back to lunch at the Welcome Hotel and said to me, 'I've fixed for you, Anne, to crew for One-eyed Jimmy in the sailing race this afternoon.' 'Does he know that I've never sailed before?' I asked. 'That doesn't matter,' he said, 'you'll soon get the hang of it.' We arrived at the harbour, where One-eyed Jimmy (I cannot remember his real name, but he did only have one eye, hence the nickname) was preparing his beloved dinghy. He looked far from pleased when daddy drove off and I confessed my ignorance of even the names used for rigging etc. The first mistake I made was to pull the wrong sheet, so it came out of its fastening at the top of the mast and the sail crashed down on top of us. One-eyed Jimmy then tried to climb the mast and we very nearly capsized. By this time the race had started and I was truly in the doghouse. Though in later year I sometimes sailed off Hayling Island with a naval cousin, Ralph Fisher I always preferred the tennis court except for picnics, which Sheila and I went on with various escorts. Sheila on the other hand, often sailed in daddy's dinghy, though I suspect most of the work was done by her numerous and devoted boy friends.

During this period we made friends with some of the tea planters and stayed with them on their plantations in the mountains that rise in the centre of Ceylon. It was wonderful to get away from the heat of the coast and enjoy the cool nights and lovely gardens in the hills. One friend Hazel was lady champion of tennis in Ceylon, and that Easter of 1939 very kindly asked me to partner with her in the forthcoming tournament. I was thrilled and stayed with her and her husband practising, before we went to Newara Eliya for the event. They drove me down to Kandy the lovely former capital, on Good Friday to meet my family who had been fishing. I began to feel very ill and by the time we reached the Hill Club in Newara Eliya, I had developed a high temperature with terrible diarrhea. It was the most virulent form of dysentery. Mummy and daddy drove me straight down to a nursing home in Colombo, a nightmare four-hour drive through monsoon rain, which I would not like to repeat. My championship hopes were over!

A few weeks later we went to the Service hill station at Diyatalawa. While we were there we rented a house from a retired planter, who moved out. It had sounded delightful, when my mother booked it over the telephone. It had a lovely garden, set among the hills. However when we arrived, we found that while the owners who had numerous dogs which they had taken with them, the dogs had left all their fleas behind and the house was infested. Moreover, the husband had been a notable *shikari* (big game hunter). There must have been thirty or forty tiger and bear heads scowling down at us, as well as stuffed smaller creatures in glass cases. Two enormous elephant tusks were displayed on either side of the doorway and there was a huge ebony and ivory screen, depicting the Taj Mahal in the drawing room. Besides these, elephant trunks upheld every lamp and waste-paper baskets were made from their feet. Altogether it was a horrific welcome to our holiday home. With her usual cheerful efficiency my mother set the servants to work, cleaning the infestations, then moving all the elephant trunks etc., and having them stacked behind the Taj Mahal screen across the opening to the square hall. The Head Boy who had been left behind, she conciliated by explaining that we wanted to preserve many of his master's treasures. All was well and the house really looked very nice, until one day the owner turned up unexpectedly to see if we were comfortable. However, my mother cleverly never allowed him into the house but diplomatically ordered tea in the garden!

This month was an idyllic period before the outbreak of the Second World War. There were many young naval officers at Diyatalawa and Sheila and I went to lots of dances. There was also a small golf course there, mostly constructed on the only level ground in the hills. As this was also used for polo matches and for the soldiers to practice hand grenade throwing, it had its excitements. Sheila and I happily played golf against each other. As we were equally bad we did not mind how many shots we took for each hole.

6

War in Ceylon

As soon as the navy was mobilized at the end of August 1939 my father was appointed Naval Officer in Charge, Trincomalee. He was given an official house there, Pellew House in the old inner dockyard. We drove right through the night from Colombo for him to take command with the rank of Commander. He was the Senior Officer on the Station, taking precedence over the Colonel and the Wing Commander at China Bay, since the navy is the senior service. It was the beginning of four of some of the happiest years in my life, and certainly in his.

The Dutch had built Pellew House in the late eighteenth century, for they had occupied Ceylon before Britain. Many of the leading Ceylonese were descended from these colonists, who had intermarried with local girls and were always known as Burghers. Indeed many of their names were Dutch. It was a charming and delightfully cool house, built nearly at the top of the hill overlooking the inner dockyard, with the completely land-locked harbour beyond. My father kept his telescope on the wall of the drawing room so that he could see whatever was happening in the port. It was a bungalow with a large drawing room, an even larger dining room, which we sometimes used for dances and three bedrooms. These rooms had long verandas on either side, with a lawn facing the harbour and a small garden with flowering trees on the roadside. The kitchens were separate. These verandas provided double roofing and so kept the rooms cool, as there was always a through draft. In any case, Trinco had a much pleasanter climate than Colombo, as we did not get the southwest monsoon, which made the latter so sticky in May and June. The rooms had no doors, but only bamboo slats across the centre, which gave minimal privacy but plenty of air to the rooms.

As Pellew House was built on the edge of the jungle we quite often had visits from snakes, monkeys, tarantulas and scorpions. Sheila once stepped on one of these, but someone killed it before it had time to sting her. Another time I went into the bathroom to wash my hands and disturbed a krait, one of the most dangerous, though smallest of the snakes, which was snoozing along the top of the open door. There was a horrid hiss and it jumped over my head into the lavatory basin. I cowered in the corner and yelled for help. Luckily it gave me a nasty look, leaped on the sponge rail over the bath, and escaped through a hole in the floor. Usually though, daddy killed any snakes with his hockey stick.

When we arrived at Trinco we found that there was a stupid and very snobbish barrier among the dockyard staff, who were divided into three grades. The social divisions in the civilian naval staff, which came under my father, were most unhappy and unnecessary and my parents immediately began to break them down. They had many dinner and drink parties, inviting everyone, at different times, from all grades, who they thought would have interests in common. My mother set up a sewing party at Pellew House making things for the war effort. I cannot quite think what we made and I am sure now, they would be quite redundant, but they brought all the wives together for a chat, coffee etc. and everyone got to know one another. They all found they had much in common, and soon everyone in the dockyard was a friend. Then daddy started up a mixed hockey club, in which he and I both played. I played as centre forward and he as a back. Very soon the naval side of Trinco was a very happy place and remained so. We also used to give supper parties for the naval ratings. Daddy used to play skittles; Sheila and I played table tennis with the younger sailors; while the Chief Yeoman of Signals gallantly partnered mother at darts. I think she very rarely even hit the board, but the parties seem to have been much enjoyed.

Pellew House, Trincomalee, with its harbour, Ceylon

Sheila and I and the two other unmarried girls were enrolled as cipher officers in the Naval Office. We worked on four-hour watches and were on call at night when secret messages came through from Colombo on the teleprinter. These were tapped out there on a sort of typewriter and then they chugged out at Trinco some two hundred miles away on thin strips of paper, which were pasted down on signal pads. The whole secrecy scheme was in fact ludicrous. The signalmen, who had mostly been in the navy all their lives, always knew exactly what was going on from the tenor of the non-secret messages. For example, when the *Queen Mary* and the *Queen Elizabeth* came into Trinco harbour to transfer ANZAC troops from the ships from that continent to the *Queens*, for onward passage to the Middle East, there were endless open signals for victualling thousands of men and everything else needed, so it was not difficult for these highly trained ratings to guess what was afoot. Moreover when we cipher officers were summoned during the night, we arrived to find that the kind signalmen had taken down our messages!

The commodores of the two *Queens* often entertained us and it was fascinating being shown over these vast ships. Trinco was the only harbour I think in the world, where they could swing at anchor. Moreover, as it is completely land-locked they were never in danger of attack. None of the troops were allowed ashore, but occasionally one swam across to the consternation of his officers. The *Queens* were so fast and possessed radar, so if they sighted any other vessel they immediately sailed in the opposite direction, as they had the speed of any ship in the world.

In return for the commodores' hospitality I once drove them up to visit the ruined city of Sigiriya. This was built on the top of an impregnable rock, towering over the surrounding flat jungle. At one point, on the way up you had to manoeuvre outwards to reach the summit, but this had now been made a bit easier. Even so, it was quite a climb and there was also a danger of being attacked by swarms of wild bees. The palace had been built for protection by a fratricidal king. It had not ultimately saved him as he was eventually murdered too. Hopefully, I also wanted to show my guests the wild animals in the jungle. On this expedition we saw a crocodile, a bird of paradise and two elephants. Our visitors were not a bit surprised but it was quite rare to see wild life in the jungle. Now of course there are game reserves.

Another day we were entertained at dinner on the *Queen Mary*. All was delightful until the time to leave arrived. Then we found that an oiler had come alongside the giant ship, while we were eating. This necessitated mother, Sheila, and me crossing the very dirty tanker in long evening dresses and climbing down her side by an iron upright ladder to daddy's bobbing motorboat in the sea below. Quite frightening enough for the uninitiated but horrific in unsuitable clothes!

In May 1940 we were up at Diyatalawa for a week's holiday. I had a dream which I told the family at breakfast, that I had seen the printed headlines in the paper - GERMANY INVADES BELGIUM, HOLLAND, AND LUXEMBOURG - later that day (remember we were some six hours ahead of GMT) the news came through that the phoney war was over. The Germans indeed had invaded these three countries. Certainly, we were all expecting an invasion but no one thought the Germans would attack Holland or Luxembourg. We sat glued to my radio all the long days of the Battle of France. I kept a map with flags

The Iron Gate, Sigiriya, Ceylon

to show the position of the armies, but as all my flags combined on the beaches of Dunkirk, my map plotting ended. I never repeated the exercise even when our troops marched triumphantly across Europe in 1944-5.

A number of our cousins were at Dunkirk. James Harden was picked up swimming about with a pound note in his mouth. (Dr.) Jock Lord (whose wedding I have described earlier) stayed, tending the wounded and only left with the survivors when German tanks arrived at the farm he had requisitioned as a field hospital. They managed to reach one of the last boats. For this he was awarded the DSO. Another cousin on my mother's side Ralph Fisher was in command of the *Wakeful*. The destroyer delivered 639 troops to safety in Dover, then another 640 off Dunkirk's beaches. Sadly they were torpedoed and sank in 15 seconds on the return journey. Ralph had a miraculous escape and clambered on board a fishing vessel, the *Comfort*, but was washed back into the sea before being rescued by a Norwegian vessel the *Hird*. He ended his career as an admiral.

A nun, Lucy Brodie's sister and an old friend of my mother had an adventurous escape from Bruges in the summer of 1940. As a British citizen her Mother Superior ordered Nina (Sister Anne) and two other foreigners to try and find a ship to their House in England. They set off, pushing their meagre belongings along the crowded and heavily bombed roads of Northern France. Eventually two soldiers gave them a lift in a jeep. At the coast Nina went to the Boarding Officer and asked for a passage. 'We can give you one', he said, ' but as the other sisters aren't British, we cannot take them.' 'I will not leave them behind.' answered Nina stoutly. It seemed an impasse but eventually the officer relented.

I was the only member of my family who liked listening to the radio. I had bought one when we were still living in Colombo with my pocket money in 1938. It was a Japanese make, which they were selling cheaply to the Ceylonese for propaganda purposes. It came into its own on the outbreak of war and all our dinner guests would crowd into Sheila's and my bedroom, sitting rather self-consciously, on our mosquito-netted beds, while the momentous news such as Pearl Harbor and the invasion of Russia by the Germans, came over the loud speaker. We heard too of the terrible bombing of British cities and London, where my grandmother was living. She wrote every few days to my mother and complained very little about the dangers and destructions in her street - Kensington Church Street - but complained bitterly about a mouse in her bedroom. Soon my aunt persuaded her to retreat to the West Country. We heard too, that all the furniture, silver, etc. that we had left stored in London had been destroyed.

Strangely enough, despite the many disasters in other theatres of war until the entry of Japan after Pearl Harbor in December 1941, Sheila and I had a wonderful time. We did our ciphering on watches of about four hours a day, then I played tennis and Sheila usually went sailing. In the evenings there were dinner parties. Many naval ships visited Trinco and we would entertain their officers and they, in return, would invite us to dine on board their ships and once we were asked to watch the aircraft landing on the *Eagle*. So many tragically were not to survive the war. The

Glorious, the *Eagle*, the *Hermes* and *Repulse*, and many more, were to be sunk all too soon.

The captain of the *Hermes*, Richard Onslow, once told us at dinner some very amusing stories about the time when he commanded the Royal Yacht, the *Victoria and Albert*. He was lucky enough to be in command during the reign of the three kings: George V, Edward VIII with Mrs Simpson, and George VI. One Sunday when George V was alive, they had divisions and the chaplain announced one of the hymns as 540-Fight the good fight-one of the King's favourites. To his fury it turned out to be another hymn. It was a different new hymnbook. He summoned the chaplain and barked 'Am I or am I not Defender of the Faith, so how do you dare to change the hymns without telling me?' Under Edward VIII, Richard was sitting next to Mrs Simpson at dinner and he was in a quandary as to how to behave. If he was too charming - actually he was a very charming man - the King looked daggers, but if he seemed to ignore her Edward thought she was being slighted! The summer following George VI's coronation, the royal party was hanging over the taffrail (sternrail) to welcome the arrival of the Duke of Gloucester. He emerged from the motorboat attired from head to foot in what Gieves or some other top outfitter, had deemed suitable attire for a royal cruise, cap, blazer and all brand new. The brothers shouted down at him, 'Harry you look absurd. You must change all those clothes!' ' No,' Prince Henry replied, 'I've bought them for the cruise, and what I've bought, I will wear.' And he climbed on board unabashed.

I remember the *Glorious* was due to enter Trinco on Christmas morning accompanied by two destroyers. Daddy had instructed his elderly but very punctilious, lieutenant to be prepared and we four went to church. The garrison church in Fort Frederick had been erected by the Dutch and with their habitual skill in architecture had built it open, with columns on either side, the northern side facing the sea. Suddenly, in the middle of the service we saw three ships, obviously the *Glorious* and her consorts sailing out to sea. My father rushed back to the Naval Office to discover from Lt. King what had happened. 'They gave the wrong password,' he replied doggedly, 'so I closed the boom.' Daddy sent his second-in-command, Dick Russell, out to the *Glorious*, which had by now been allowed to enter the harbour. A livid Captain D'Oyley Hughes confronted poor Dick. Luckily, it was the *Glorious's* signalman who had been at fault. I never now hear the carol, 'I see three ships come sailing in on Christmas day in the morning....' without thinking of that Christmas morning of 1940.

As there were no civilian pilots at Trinco, daddy, a naval navigator, used to bring the occasional merchantman into harbour. He much enjoyed this. Merchant captains are not allowed, however experienced by their insurances, to do this themselves. Usually, they would have been quite competent but my father said one old captain only had a child's atlas to guide him around the world.

One time father piloted in a Norwegian ship and casually asked her captain and another officer to a drink at our house that evening. 'I'll send my motorboat at 6pm,' he said. When he told us at lunch, I volunteered with Sheila, to drive down to the jetty to pick them up. The motorboat arrived and two men alighted. I went up to them and said, 'the car is here.' I thought they looked a bit surprised but they followed me and got into the car. As we started up Sheila addressed them in slow English, 'Norway must be a very beautiful country?' 'I suppose so,' answered one of the men, 'but I've never been there!' We had picked up the wrong passengers. Sheila and I were so convulsed by laughter that we could not speak. By this time we had arrived home and daddy came out to greet the 'captain', only to find these two were British army officers on passage to India. They had seen a boat and had jumped in before the Norwegian captain had finished changing his clothes! All was explained, the Norwegian captain was rescued from another jetty and a jolly if enlarged party took place.

Prince Philip a midshipman at that time came to Trinco on a fortnight's surveying project. It was just before Italy invaded Greece in 1940 and at that time the Admiralty did not want a Greek prince as he then was, to be engaged in a battle against the Italians. (Later, however, he took part against them in the Battle of Matapan.) Naturally, he was much annoyed at being put ashore at such a time. He often came to the house. I remember he was particularly good at chatting with some of the Highland deep-sea fisherman, who manned the boom defence and we were also entertaining to drinks. Many years later mother told me that daddy had said to her then, 'What a wonderful husband Philip would make for Princess Elizabeth.'

Sheila had her twenty-first birthday in January 1941 and the captain of the *Eagle* gave her a dance on board. As Japan was not yet in the war there was no blackout and it was a wonderfully festive occasion, as the navy has a tradition of running such parties superbly. Luckily, we were not to know, the tragic end of this ship and so many of her crew eighteen months later.

7

Buddha's Rays

After Pearl Harbor on 7 December 1941 war had reached our zone. Suddenly Trincomalee became a major port. It was now decided that the Naval Office in Trinco must be expanded. There were not many women left in Trinco, for all those with small children were evacuated, mostly to East Africa or Australia, but daddy interviewed those that were left. One was turned down because she was an alcoholic, and another a senior officer's wife, because she was known not to be trusted with confidential documents. Not because she was a traitor, but because she was garrulous! We were a mixed bunch, a sort of ladies' Dad's Army. Some of the wives had been expert pre-war secretaries and could rattle off letters with great skill, while others were elderly and could only be trusted to sort papers.

However, before this new office at Trinco was set up, Sheila and I, and the other two regulars were sent down to the head Naval Office at Colombo. We stayed with friends there. The Colombo cipher office was very large and there were about twenty girls on each watch. (Wrens did not come to Ceylon until much later, as, at this time it was considered too dangerous. I suppose we who were already there, were expendable!) We worked on four-hour shifts throughout the twenty-four hours. At night we were picked up by cars and just put a cotton housecoat over our nighties. Unfortunately this came to the ears of the admiral, the newly appointed Commander-in-Chief Sir Geoffrey Layton. He then put out a special signal stating that we should be properly attired. How a cotton housecoat differed from a cotton dress, I have yet to fathom. I think the idea of the nightie must have shocked his naval correctness.

One horrifying incident I learned from another cipherette in Colombo, made me in later years never worry too much about small mistakes in the post-war world. One night two of the girls working in pairs decoding, received a message from a sinking merchantman in the Indian Ocean giving her position at the time of the attack. This was relayed to the Eastern Fleet, but both girls had failed to notice that they had given the position as so many degrees west, not east. The entire fleet changed course in the wrong direction until the pocket battleship (which I think it was,) sank another ship. We all had to initial the signals we decoded and the two miserable cipherettes were hauled before the admiral and shown the disastrous telegram. They would never forget that night and how a second's carelessness, or probably, tiredness could cost so many lives.

The Japanese were now beginning to advance down the Malay Peninsula. It was at this juncture that Churchill sent the *Prince of Wales* and the *Repulse* to Singapore. The *Prince of Wales* stopped in Colombo and the *Repulse* in Trinco her captain, Captain Tennant, stayed with us at Pellew House for a few days on their way east. He was a charming man, who loved watching the birds in our garden. Many of his midshipmen came up to the house, some of them only seventeen, and played ping-pong with Sheila and me. Two weeks later many of them were dead after the Japanese sank the two ships off Malaya. Captain Tennant went down with his ship. I remember my father was horrified when he first heard that two battleships were being sent without air cover, which was against every naval strategy. He was the first person, I heard, who predicted that Singapore would fall. Everyone else had gone on saying that the port was unassailable.

Singapore fell on 15 February 1942. Almost all the defenders were imprisoned or killed. The administration of Singapore during those last weeks seems to have been incompetent in the extreme. Most of those who escaped came to Ceylon and so we heard first hand of the final days of the city. The great guns were pointed seawards. Nobody seems to have conceived that the Japanese would have the skill with a smaller force, of advancing from the north. In fact, they did not need even to penetrate the thick jungle but appear to have marched down the main highway, largely unopposed. I remember, a captain of a merchantman (a retired naval officer), one of the last to leave the stricken port, telling me in a fury not only how he had seen the guns still facing the wrong way, but later had witnessed Australian and other troops pushing aside women and children to secure places for themselves in the last ships before the surrender.

One army officer I met at a party some weeks later, (there were still lots of parties), told me that he had been badly wounded in the leg but had been rescued by his batman. They escaped in a motorboat to Batavia. The enemy heavily strafed them and the others with them were all killed. On arrival the two men were advised to cross the island, as the Japanese were about to arrive here too. They struggled across the mountain range, through thick jungle, to find the enemy was already on the other side. They took to a boat again but in Sumatra it was the same story. They managed to board the last ship - an old paddle steamer and set sail for Ceylon. My acquaintance was standing on deck - there was no other space - when they saw the conning tower of a submarine and then the line of an advancing torpedo, aimed directly at their ship. He thought 'This is it!' Nothing happened. The submarine dived but her aim had been too low. Her captain had not realized she was a paddle steamer and the torpedo had passed beneath her. My friend then said he was sorry he had come to another island!

Although the defence of Singapore had been so appallingly mishandled, service personnel from there were always saying, 'this is not how we did it in Singapore.' One was interrupted by my father, who said, 'We do not wish to hear what you did in Singapore!' Another man boasted he had been playing golf when the city fell. 'Just like Drake before the Armada!' 'But hardly the same outcome,' retorted daddy.

It was about this time that we saw in Trinco the unusual sunset, known as the Buddha's Rays. This was a sunset in the east, a reflection of the true sunset in the west. On this occasion it appeared even more like the Japanese flag as white rays appeared from the crimson skyline. I think we all secretly felt that it was a bad omen.

With the capture of the Far East, Trinco became a boomtown. From a comparatively quiet outpost of Empire almost overnight, its harbour was filled with men-of-war, supply ships and Indian army contingents took over the army base at Fort Frederick. The air base at China Bay, at the other side of the harbour, was also expanded as much as possible. We saw little of them. I was seconded for a fortnight or so to help them with their deciphering. I can mostly remember being harassed by their pet mongoose, which kept playfully biting my heels. This tiny air force was later to play a decisive part in the defeat of Japanese aggression in the Bay of Bengal.

Sheila and I were working very hard with about five ladies under us, whose ages ranged from about 18 (my age) to sixtyish. Every ship seemed to be sending signals unendingly, which all passed through our hands. They had either to be enciphered or deciphered, or sent by teleprinter to Colombo. To make copies to be distributed around, we used a carbon paper called ormig. It was purple and came off on our hands. We then got hot - by this time all the offices were blacked out - and we rubbed the sweat off our faces and ended up purple!

Admiral Palliser had now taken over in Trinco, and under him Captain Bell, who had won renown with HMS *Exeter* at the Battle of the River Plate. Both these men were of course, senior to my father, but I do not believe that they ever even considered turning us out of Pellew House, though they often dined with us. Daddy was now appointed King's Harbour Master, an office, given to Navigation Officers, and a position my father had always longed for.

8

The Most Dangerous Moment of the War

In March 1946 Lester Pearson, then Canadian Ambassador to the United States and later Prime Minister of Canada, told how at a lunch party in the embassy in Washington, over coffee a guest asked Sir Winston Churchill who was on a visit, what he considered the most dangerous moment in the war had been, and what had caused him the most alarm? Churchill answered, to their great surprise, that it was when the news was received that the Japanese fleet had entered the Bay of Bengal and was heading for Ceylon. Sir Arthur Bryant in *The Turn of the Tide* reiterated this, writing that 'a naval victory in April 1942 would have given Japan control of the Indian Ocean, isolated the Middle East, and brought down the Churchill government.'

Singapore fell on 15 February and the next day Admiral Raeder, the German Commander-in-Chief, in a report to Hitler wrote: 'Japan plans to protect this front in the Indian Ocean by capturing the key position of Ceylon, and she also plans to gain control of the sea in that area by means of superior naval forces. 15 Japanese submarines are at that moment operating in the Bay of Bengal, in the waters off Ceylon and in the straits on both sides of Sumatra and Java...
Once Japanese battleships, aircraft carriers and submarines and the Japanese Air Force are based on Ceylon, Britain will be forced to resort to heavily escorted convoys if she desires to maintain communications with India and the Near East.'

The Japanese, under Admiral Nagumo Chuichi, who had had operational command at Pearl Harbor, had first envisaged a grand plan of capturing Ceylon and then, with the aid of Japanese ground forces of five divisions, linking with the Germans advancing from the Caucasus. The Japanese High Command rejected this plan. However, had the British Eastern

Fleet been sunk in Colombo and Trincomalee harbours it is very possible that Admiral Nagumo would have seized Ceylon as a base to attack our ships and forces in the Bay of Bengal and the Indian Ocean.

On 8th March the First Sea Lord sent a warning to Churchill that Ceylon was now threatened. Its loss 'would undermine our whole position in the Middle East as well as the Far East.' A new Commander-in-Chief, Sir James Somerville, was appointed to command the Eastern Fleet and Sir Geoffrey Layton became Commander-in-Chief Ceylon. Sir James was ordered to use the old battleships *Ramillies* and *Royal Sovereign* to protect the island. Sir James replied that without air cover, there would be a repetition of the sinking of the *Prince of Wales* and *Repulse*. 'If the Japs launched an attack with their full strength captured Ceylon and destroy the greater part of the Eastern Fleet (as at Pearl Harbor)... the situation becomes really desperate.' On 26 March Sir Dudley Pound ordered Sir James not to allow his fleet to become engaged with anything except inferior forces until the Eastern Fleet could be reinforced. Sir James now had his orders. He must try and do as much to damage the enemy as possible but not to lose his fleet. The situation in some ways is parallel to that when the Drake faced the Spanish Armada in the sixteenth century. His much smaller ships attacked the Spaniards with their greater manoeuvrability and better gunnery, rather than at close range. Then he sent in his fire ships, which did terrible damage, before harrying them around our coasts until the storms off Scotland completed their destruction. Queen Elizabeth I acknowledged this with her commemorative medal - He blew and they were scattered - Admiral Somerville was aided by more modern friends unknown to Drake and his seamen, the cipher breakers and secret agents, and as Churchill acknowledged, the bravery of the crew of an antiquated Catalina.

On paper Sir James' fleet was formidable - 5 battleships, 3 aircraft carriers, 11 cruisers, 16 destroyers, and 3 submarines. But these were scattered, running out of oil and water, and many in desperate need of a refit. Moreover, they had never operated together before. Not only this, but until the first signal from secret reports of Japanese movements, he did not know the size or position of the enemy fleet, nor of its intentions, whereas they knew most of the whereabouts of the British fleet and the number of the defending planes. Though the Japanese could not decipher our codes, they had innumerable spies in India and

Ceylon who provided them with information. They hoped to find our ships in Colombo and Trinco harbours, as at Pearl Harbor and the few planes grounded, and so easy to destroy on the ground. But they did not have three pieces of information, which were to prove vital to us in the coming weeks. They never knew of the hastily constructed new runway on the race course in Colombo, from which aircraft were to defend Ceylon so gallantly; secondly, they do not appear, from later Japanese sources, to have had any knowledge of the secret oiling station at Addu Atoll, a ring of coral islands surrounding a deep water lagoon some six hundred miles SSE of Ceylon; finally they were unaware that Sir James knew their movements. An intelligence group, which had been formed in Singapore, but had luckily been evacuated to Colombo before the capture of that city, discovered the outline of the Japanese plans. They formed the nucleus of a new radio intercept station, now an inclusively naval unit (Y). This unit consisted of naval radio operators, interpreters, and cryptanalysts and 38 WRNS. It appears that both our and the American decoders were able to break JN25, a five digit code which gave them the vital information on the Japanese fleet movement in March 1942.

The Japanese fleet left Celebes on 31 March, under the command of Admiral Nagumo. His striking force consisted of 5 fleet carriers, 4 battleships, 2 heavy cruisers and a light cruiser, 11 destroyers, and more than 300 aircraft. They were supported by tankers and supply ships, which refuelled their fleet before it entered the Bay of Bengal. In addition Vice-Admiral Ozawa in command of the Malaya force, consisting of 6 cruisers, a carrier, and 8 destroyers attacked shipping in the Bay of Bengal and caused enormous panic down the eastern Indian seaboard. The Japanese boosted by their successes in Malaya were in no doubt of the strength of their position. 'The use of such a powerful aircraft Task Force for the destruction of the British fleet in the Indian Ocean was a case of using a sledgehammer to break an egg.'(Captain Keizo. *The Tragedy of Vice-Admiral Nagumo*).

Sir James was in a dilemma. He had been warned by intelligence on 28 March to expect an attack about 1 April. He therefore gathered his scattered fleet to the south of Ceylon ready to attack the enemy at night. For three days and two nights he waited, while his ships were running out of oil and water. He described his feelings in a talk he gave to the BBC in 1944:

'We did not know in what strength the Japanese would stage this attack. We anticipated a cut and run operation by a force consisting of two or three battleships and a couple of carriers escorted by some cruisers and destroyers. We rather expected the Japanese aircraft would attack at dawn (so that they could land on their carriers in daylight), and that the Japanese would then make an immediate get-away to the Eastward, in order to avoid attack by the British land-based aircraft in Ceylon.'

Sir James divided his fleet into two, Force 'A', the fast ships, under his immediate orders, and Force 'B' under Vice-Admiral Willis, to search for the enemy. On the evening of 2 April he decided that the signal must have been mistaken. He decided to sail for Addu Atoll, sending the *Dorsetshire* and *Cornwall* to Colombo and the *Hermes* and *Vampire* to Trinco. He arrived at Addu Atoll on 4 April. (' a bloody awful looking place, which beats the band for an abomination of heat and desolation.') It was there that the fateful signal reached him at 1600 that a huge Japanese fleet was, indeed, sailing for Ceylon, now six hundred miles away. This is a signal I remember so well - a list of the Japanese ships, then ending 'Destination Ceylon.'

The heroic story of the captain and crew of the Catalina, which saved the Eastern Fleet, and, probably Ceylon being captured, has actually been told by members of her crew, Squadron Leader Len Birchall (a Canadian) and Sergeant Brian Catlin. Though we all thought they had been killed, happily six survived the war. Indeed, at the same lunch party with Sir Winston and Lester Pearson, which I have already mentioned, Churchill said sadly, 'That gallant pilot lies at the bottom of the Indian Ocean.' 'Not at all', answered Lester Pearson, 'he is, at this moment in Washington.' (Birchall only knew that his signal had got through to Colombo at Manila after his release from his Japanese prisoner-of-war camp.)

Birchall arrived at China Bay (Trinco) late on 2 April, but next evening he was ordered to take off for a long distance - 24 hour patrol - to the south of Ceylon. They left so hurriedly the next morning that they had no time for breakfast and there was only a little food and water in the plane, which had been left over from Karachi, their previous base. Nor had they been warned about the Japanese fleet. Their orders were to make a sweep some 250 miles SSE of Ceylon. In the event, they luckily patrolled further, because the moon was so bright. At about 500 nautical miles south of Ceylon they started to turn. Suddenly the keen-eyed Sergeant Colarossi thought he saw something on the horizon. They went in to get closer, to fix the position, and to investigate, for they still thought they were our own ships.

As they approached Birchall wrote, 'There were more specks and then they started to take form. Obviously they were warships...what we saw were 4 battleships, 5 aircraft carriers, with cruisers, and destroyers. We still could not see enough of the fleet to justify an assumption of nationality as the number we saw was less than the number given to us in the Allied naval section. Just as we started our transmission 6 flights of 3 Zeros each peeled off over the top of us and we were into it...once we were close enough to identify them as Japanese, it was too late. We did a hurried count and set up a first sighting message.' To their surprise instead of attacking the Catalina, the Japs waved merrily at the Allied crew, for they had been told to expect a captured Catalina to lead them into Ceylon. This gave Birchall's signaller Fred Phillips, time to send back to Colombo his vital message. At this moment the Japanese realized their mistake and opened fire on the almost defenceless Catalina. Colarossi was hit and killed. Meanwhile Phillips sent out the priority code in clear, 'O-Break-O'. The Catalina caught fire, and despite the manoeuvring the pilot attempted and the desperate firing from their few guns, Birchall was forced to ditch the plane. All the surviving eight crew members were in the sea, heavily strafed by the Japs. Henzell and Davidson died in the water. Then to their amazement, they saw a whaler approaching. They were taken to the destroyer, the *Isokaze*, Birchall was savagely beaten and so were the others. The Japanese then heard Colombo asking for a repeat of the signal and realized that there was nothing further to find out. The three least wounded were still continually beaten, but they made up a story that they had just come from India. They were later transferred to the

IJN Isokase that picked up Birchall's crew after the Zeros have shot them down on 4 April (Courtesy Air Cdr. Birchall)

flagship, where Birchall and his crew discovered Phillip's diary and ate it page by page. Surprisingly on board the *Akagi* the wounded were given first class attention, but once in Japan, barbarous treatment began again. However all six survived the war.

A naval signalman at Colombo took down the vital signal. 'We picked up the message, which did sound garbled but we got it down. When we saw what it was the place went deathly quiet and for a heck of a long time.' It was immediately passed on to Sir James at Addu Atoll. Admiral Sir Geoffrey Layton realized that the attack was likely next day, Easter Sunday, and cleared the harbour of the remaining ships. Vice-Admiral Arbuthnot had already reduced their number when the original signal had arrived. During the night reports were received of cruisers and battleships but the aircraft carriers were not seen, probably due to lowering skies. The not very effective radar at Colombo reported aircraft at 0740 on Easter Sunday 5 April. The attack came at 0800. The attacking force consisted of 92 bombers and 36 fighters. They dive-bombed and machine-gunned the harbour, but only the refitting *Tenedos* and an unarmed merchant cruiser were sunk, and the submarine depot ship the *Lucia* was holed. Meanwhile, though the warning time had been so short, our pilots were already in their cockpits. 42 fighters and 14 Hurricanes, from the newly created airstrip on Colombo racecourse, took off to engage the enemy. A fierce battle took place over the harbour. By 0835 all the enemy planes had gone. We shot down 9 certains and more probables. (The RAF claimed 19 certains and more probables.) We lost 21 Catalinas, Fulmars and Hurricanes, as well as 6 defenceless Swordfish on their way from Trinco to Ratmalana, who sadly ran into the enemy fighters over Colombo harbour. The pilot of one of the ditched Hurricanes came to the surface to find the Japanese Lieut. Ibusuki Masanobi waving to him and calling out: 'See you again in the future in some other sky!'

Now where would the Japanese fleet go? They turned south and at 1355 sank the *Dorsetshire* and *Cornwall* in a few minutes. Admiral Somerville sent destroyers to pick up survivors, 1,122, but both captains and 422 men were lost. Sir James did not know whether the Japanese would now attack Trinco or Addu Atoll. Nagumo searched for the Eastern Fleet. They were, in fact, not far apart but he never discovered it. Admiral of the Fleet Sir Algernon Willis wrote later in his memoirs:

'Had the fleet not had to return to Addu on 4th April because of water shortage in the 3rd Battle Squadron we would have continued cruising south to southwestward of Ceylon and must have been located by the enemy on 5th April with their five carriers to our two (not properly trained). This would have been disaster to the Eastern Fleet by air attack before the battleships made contact, and it is not difficult to imagine what would have happened when they did.'

On the afternoon of 8 April the only serviceable Catalina L for Leonard, sighted the huge Japanese fleet 400 miles east of Ceylon steering directly for Trincomalee. Admiral Layton immediately ordered Trinco harbour to be evacuated. That night my father and the navigator of *HMS Hermes*, the only pilots available, were ordered to clear the harbour of all shipping including *HMS Vampire*.

L for Leonard was able to escape the Japanese fighters in the clouds and returned to base with the news of the enemy numbers. We had only 17 Hurricanes and 6 Fulmars to meet the 91 Kate bombers and 38 Zero fighters but these gallantly set out to meet the attackers. 8 Hurricanes and 3 Fulmars were shot down. They shot down 15, and AA accounted for 9. More of the enemy planes were damaged.

The 9th of April was a beautiful morning. I was on early morning watch with another girl and the naval cipher lieutenant at the Naval Office in the Inner Dockyard at Trinco. I happened to be on the balcony of the one-storey building, when I heard a massive drone of aeroplane engines. 'Oh good', I thought, 'I didn't know we had so many!' At that moment the first bombs fell. A stick straddled the office and there was a great splash in the harbour just below where I was standing. I dived under the office desk, with the other two, and the windows blew out. It was 0725. The raid must have lasted about half an hour. The planes began by bombing, and then systematically machine-gunned the houses at low level. Our house, Pellew House, had holes in every ceiling. Daddy had returned there for breakfast and a shave, having been out all night piloting the ships from the harbour. Mummy and Sheila were there too, waiting for their turns to go on watch. Happily nobody was hurt and a large silver framed mirror, which I am looking at as I write, stayed serenely on its table untouched by the attack. Luckily no bombs fell on the arsenal, which was just below Pellew House. The raid was described in the Japanese Official History as a 'spectacular display of fireworks.'

When the bombing stopped the lieutenant told me and the other girl to go to a makeshift shelter in the Inner Yard. The Naval Office had been missed but almost every other building there had been damaged or destroyed. Wounded and dead were lying everywhere, scattered over the roads. It was the only time in the war that I saw casualties, though I was in central London from July 1943-45. As we walked towards the shelter I saw some sick berth stewards carrying wounded into a nearby warehouse. We stopped and asked if they would like any help? They gratefully agreed and we went into a back room and tried to bind up wounds etc. None of my limited First Aid courses had prepared me for what we were faced with. All our patients were Tamils and knew very little English so they could not tell us where their injuries were. Also it was very difficult to see them as the men were coated in red mud or dust from the fallen buildings in which they had been trapped. We had no water, but a sick berth attendant brought us some in a bowl, and we dabbed rather ineffectively at enormous gashes and covered them with bandages. The only injury I treated properly was a broken collarbone, which I remembered how to deal with from one of my classes. We tried to talk encouragingly but these poor men must have been so mystified by this completely unexpected and horrifying air attack that they were in a state of shock. After about half an hour they were taken away to hospital. By this time my father and the other officers had appeared, as well as my relief, so I thankfully drove home.

The Japanese had flown away but we expected them back at any moment. The Inner Yard was in chaos, with most of the buildings damaged and several ships on fire in the harbour. As the electricity had been cut all food in the fridges was quickly going bad. Several hundred Tamil workmen were killed during the raid, but sadly they were never identified and no relation ever asked for them. Peter Irwin, the Police Chief had the bodies loaded on to a lorry, but where were they to be buried? He asked for help from the Indian Army colonel at Fort Frederick. He was a bit doubtful, as his troops were all Muslims and would be contaminated if they touched a dead Hindu or Buddhist. 'Oh, they are all good Moslems.' Peter lied stoutly and the reluctant soldiers bore them away. The monitor *Erebus* and the *SS Saigang* were damaged and were later both beached (by my father) but the *Saigang* was a total loss. Meanwhile, nine RAF Blenheim light bombers had taken off at 0840 to attack the Japanese carriers. The Japanese were taken completely by surprise and though six bombs fell near the *Akagi* no damage was caused. Six of the gallant nine were shot down. (The numbers of the allied and enemy planes taking part and shot down differ slightly in the different official documents.) 'A useless sacrifice,' Willis remarked. But a Japanese said of the incident, that it was the first time their fleet had been attacked since Pearl Harbor.

My watch ended, I drove up the hill to Pellew House to find chaos. The air attack on the house had left tiles from the roof everywhere and I suppose there were a good many pieces of furniture damaged. However, nothing daunted, mother was supervising the servants as they reluctantly swept up the debris after which they vanished. Before the Raid, as it was always called, some 19,000 had been employed in the dockyard, next day 120 men turned up. The electricity and telephone lines had been destroyed, so there was only dried food in tins and troops had to be sent to Trinco market, wearing gas masks, to clear the rotting meat and other food. All the local population had disappeared, either by trains, bus, lorries, ox carts, or on foot into the jungle or to other parts of the island. The only one of our servants who returned a month later was David, the cook, who explained apologetically that he had only taken his wife and children to safety and then come back. Sadly one of his children had died in the crush of the panic-stricken exodus.

The *Hermes* and *Vampire* sailed from Trincomalee on the morning of 9 April, but due to all the telegraph wires and electricity having been cut by the attack on China Bay they did not receive the warning signals in time. A huge force attacked them. *Hermes* sank at 1030. The *Vampire*, the corvette *Hollyhock* and two tankers were also sunk. A hospital ship the *Vita*, picked up 600 survivors, but Captains Onslow and Moran went down with their ships. This rescue operation was helped by a humane Japanese destroyer, who actually signalled the hospital ship with their positions to show where the survivors were.

Of course, no one knew that Admiral Nagumo had turned away forever. That afternoon we began digging makeshift trenches and really thought the Japanese were going to invade. I think it was the only time in the war that I was really frightened and I had nightmares for many months of Japanese bayoneting me! Actually that same afternoon, April 9 a Catalina reported a fleet of 3 carriers and 9 large vessels, accompanied by destroyers 170 miles east of Ceylon. Admiral Nagumo was making for the Malacca Straits well satisfied, his fleet seemingly almost unscathed, despite the heroic attacks by our few aircraft. However the Eastern Fleet though sadly weakened by the loss of the *Hermes, Dorsetshire, Cornwall, Vampire* and many merchantmen, had survived.

The gravity of this incursion into the Bay of Bengal has been largely forgotten and very few people are aware of the dangers of April 1942. To my mind two main events prevented a catastrophe. First the bravery of the Catalina crews, who warned the Commanders-in-Chief in time for them to clear the two harbours of shipping and alert our small band of aircraft to attack the bombers and second the Special Intelligence Organisation at Colombo, who gave Admiral Somerville warning of the impending attack on 31 March. Though Admiral Nagumo's ships were largely undamaged, he suffered heavy losses of aircraft and three of his ships had to be sent for refits. This may well have been a factor in the great victory by the Americans at the Battle of the Midway.

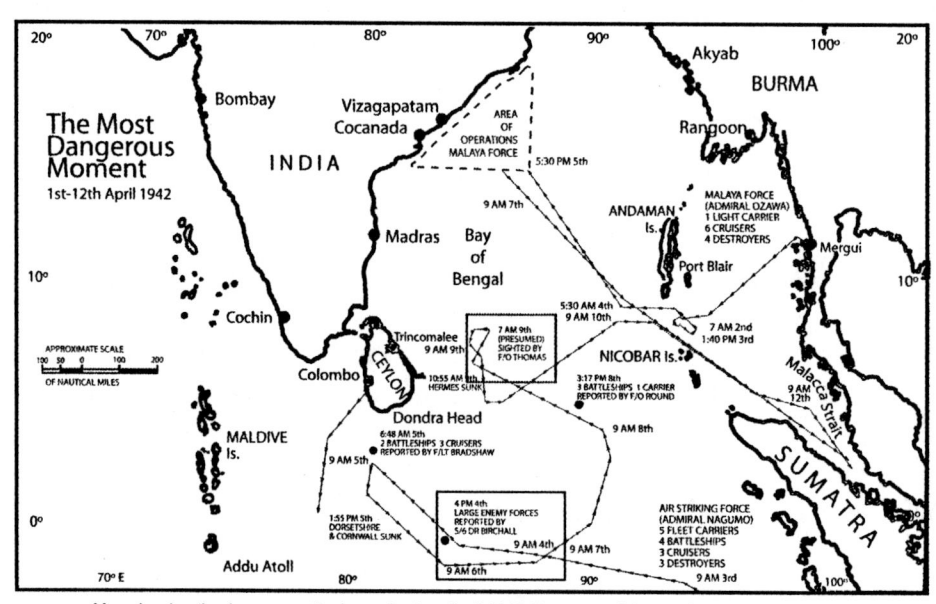

Map showing the Japanese attacks on Ceylon, April 1942 (Courtesy of the late Michael Tomlinson)

9

The Post Raid Period

Imagine what Trinco was like on the afternoon of 9 April! The Japanese aircraft had gone but we thought they would return and invade us. All the servants and Ceylonese workers had disappeared. The electricity had been cut, so there was no fresh food. All the food in the fridge had gone bad and the water was contaminated. Nor were there any lights when darkness came, about 6 pm, except for the odd candle left over from Christmas. There were no air-raid shelters of any description. The two sunken ships were still blazing in the harbour.

About 5.30 pm I said to Sheila, 'Shall we make a cup of tea?' We were alone in the house, as daddy was salvaging the ships and mother was on watch. We had left England while there were still servants in all upper-class houses, though we were never very well off, and none of us had learned to cook. (I believe mummy had cookery lessons at her school before World War I). However, Sheila and I now made our way into the empty kitchen. It was apart from the rest of the house and boasted a wood-burning stove, on which our cook made the most delicious meals. Trying to remember what we had learned as girl guides, we managed to light the fire and set an old kettle on it filled with cold water. I then noticed a small detachment of Balloon Defence men standing outside the garden on the little road on the edge of the jungle. 'I'll go and ask them if they would like a cup of tea, and perhaps we could find some biscuits somewhere?' I said to Sheila. I went out and asked the sergeant whether they would like to come in? They were delighted. They trooped into the kitchen and we chatted, while the kettle failed to come to the boil. At last in desperation I made a lukewarm brew and they ate the biscuits, which we had discovered. Anyway the men enjoyed coming into a private house, but obviously did not think much of Sheila and my cookery skills. To be fair without any milk or bread it was difficult. As they left they asked if we would like them to come down and cook breakfast for us? After that they came every morning during the emergency (which lasted a few weeks), bringing some rations with them and they cooked breakfast for us all. In return we lent them books, which helped to relieve their tedium when they were on patrol on the hill above Pellew House and they proudly showed us photos of their families.

Of course, our ciphering watches continued, but it was extremely difficult to light up the Naval Office after dark. For security reasons we had to keep a strict blackout and the office was terribly hot. We all raided our cupboards for candles, which we perched on files, which then were knocked over, when we ended a line of typing. They also added to the heat, but it was very funny. As there was no fresh food, just tins, taken from the stores, mostly tinned bully beef, tinned salmon, and, strangely enough, tinned raspberries. Particularly trying there was very little bread, for the ship carrying the flour must have been sunk, and anyway all the bakers had vanished. What did arrive had huge wet holes in the loaves. A makeshift mess was set up in Admiralty House, where Sheila had stayed with the Somervilles before the war in 1938. Here we sat at long tables eating the disgusting food. I have never been able to eat any bully beef or tinned salmon again! We must have taken some of the tins home, as I do not ever remember going to Admiralty House in the evening. Also some of the ships that came in brought us loaves of bread. Very thoughtfully the Bishop of Colombo (Cecil Horsley) came to stay for a night and brought us a hamper of food. I suppose things were not as short in Colombo by then. It was the only time in the war that I was hungry. We all lost pounds! Once the crisis was over-a month or so later-we were given much needed leave and drove up into the hills. It was like Heaven. We went to stay with our Sparling cousins on their lovely tea estate and luxuriated in hot baths and wonderful food.

In May while we were recovering from the Raid, my cousin, Molly Harden, now married to Colonel Alleyn Moore, was escaping from Burma with her nine-month old son, Patrick. She had gone out there to join her husband, Alleyn, in 1939. When the Japanese invaded Burma, she was staying in a village called Falam, the local army HQ. Alleyn was with the Falam Platoon, the Chin Hills Battalion, Burma Frontier force, but he kept sending desperate messages for her and Patrick to escape to India. However, she had an army wife staying with her Kathleen Learmond, who had a little girl Margaret aged about two, but her new baby Jean was only two months old and so they lingered as long as possible, hoping things would improve.

The situation became most grave and they were forced to leave. Molly had a Chin orderly a boy, and a local NCO as an escort. Kathleen only had a Gurkha orderly, who had loyally stayed with her when the other servants fled. Molly and Kathleen had ponies and there were mules for what baggage they could manage. A kind of palanquin was rigged up out of a bed with bamboo sticks as handles and this was carried in turn by local recruits. Kathleen put her two babies on this. Molly pushed Patrick in a pushchair up and down the rough mountain paths, or sometimes they rode on the ponies. They usually marched 15-18 miles a day, stopping at primitive rest houses for the night. These were often two-roomed shacks. They had brought tins of Horlicks, marmite, and coffee with them and bought scraggy chickens and eggs where possible, in any tiny village they passed through. At the end of the long day they had to prepare food for themselves and tend the children. Water soon ran out and they were forced to drink from the paddy fields. Molly said 'If we die, we die, but we must drink!' They were about to stop at Lake Relake when word was sent to them that Jap commandos were not far behind. They were both worried about their husbands and heard distant machine-gun fire but they were not directly attacked. Then the rains began. They and the children, who they tried to protect with tarpaulin covers, were soaked to the skin. Huge leeches - two to three inches long, striped yellow and black, attacked them. They used salt to get them off. Even small streams became formidable barriers - one had become a torrent twenty yards across. Undaunted, with the help of some villagers, they inched the bed carrying the three children across, with the foaming water up to their knees. Another three miles climb and they had reached the Indian border.

The officer commanding the Asian Rifles welcomed them with food, fires and hot baths. He even provided toys left behind by his own children. However, danger was not past. After a horrific fourteen-mile walk through torrential rain they found the river Dhaleswari was in flood. There were three tiny boats to carry them with three boatmen in each. One was for Molly, Patrick and her three dogs; Kathleen was in the next with her two children; and in the third was the orderly with the baggage. Snuggling up for warmth with the boatmen they spent the next two and half days in the boats just stopping at night, cooking on a tiny primus stove, and washing nappies in the yellow river. Poor Kathleen now went down with a chill. At last they reached Calcutta by trains and a steamer. What a contrast! They arrived at the largest hotel dishevelled and in khaki leggings, to be refused admission. 'All full, Mem Sahib'. 'No', said Molly, 'Turn out some of the subalterns and give us the best rooms.' It worked. A happy ending and both husbands joined them quite soon having escaped to fight another day.

To return to Trincomalee: Social life of a very basic sort soon started again and I have never been to so many impromptu parties and dances. There was plenty of swimming too. Moonlight picnics along the beautiful coast. There was never any problem with petrol. I had learned to drive a year or so before. I passed my test on my eighteenth birthday, the legal age in Ceylon, so I must have practised before that but nobody seemed to have minded. Daddy tried to teach Sheila, but though she was not scared, we all were as she had no idea of steering. In fact, she never learned to drive. One naval captain who was one of her many admirers, said he would be able to teach her, fathers were never any use. He took her to the local sport field the *maidan*, but after she had knocked over the goalpost he too gave up!

An unpleasant effect of the disappearance of manual labourers during the next four weeks was a virulent outbreak of black-water fever - a severe type of malaria. Before the Raid, though there were plenty of mosquitoes, which all attacked daddy and me and left Sheila and mummy alone, there were no serious epidemics. However, a few days after the Raid, because anti-mosquito sprayers treated none of the puddles, small ponds and inlets on the coast, a very serious number of troops and inhabitants came down with this disease and some died. Pam Warnett, one of the only two other unmarried girls in Trinco, got the fever and was very ill. She was very pretty but while her fever was high, her hair was shaved and the new hair came in curly and for a short time she looked very comical with some straight and some curly locks!

Another consequence of the disappearance of the locals was that the *dhobis* or washer men had left everybody's washing in their backyards. The troops, who had their washing done by these *dhobis*, began to get fed up with having no clean clothes and raided their gardens, helping themselves to the requisite number of garments they thought they were missing. One of them spied two pairs of my shorts. I remember they were decorated with little green sailing boats. One day he appeared at Pellew House with them and asked if they were mine? I was very grateful. I suppose he had seen me when I was playing hockey!

Suddenly one summer afternoon, when we were swimming with friends near Fort Frederick, someone cried out, 'The Fleet has returned!' Sure enough on the horizon and about to turn to enter Trinco Harbour, we saw the return of the Eastern Fleet, which had abandoned us for Kilindini in East Africa after the Japanese attack. They did not stay long, but it was a wonderful moment. Things were returning to normal.

During that summer we had an official visit from the then Duke of Gloucester. It was code-named Sunshine. The Prince stayed with the new Government Agent, Pat Rennison. He tried to think of everything that might be needed, but the only thing that the Prince's equerry required was some cod liver oil. Not for its usual purpose but because the Duke had something in his eye! Poor Pat also had a problem because of his lack of swimming expertise. The Prince wanted to go for a swim. He dived in and set out for a distant yacht. Pat realized he could not hope to keep up with him and gave up his attempt to be with him always. I do not know if he really found it an operation 'Sunshine'.

During the late summer my father suddenly became very ill with violent stomach pains. Mother rang the doctor, who she could tell even on the telephone, was very drunk. However, he did eventually appear but was so inebriated that he could not even find daddy's pulse. Mother was furious. She ordered him out of the house and she and I drove down to the military headquarters at Fort Frederick and asked for their doctor to attend daddy. They were rather loath to do so because of medical etiquette, but a doctor did come, organized an ambulance to the hospital in Colombo, and my father was taken there. I do not know what was the matter, but he recovered fairly soon and returned to Trinco, but the hospital advised that he had been long enough in the East and should return to England. Meanwhile, the drunken Doctor X had to appear before my father for being drunk on duty. Poor daddy, it was a ghastly position, but he got around it by saying, it was difficult for him to judge, as he had been the patient. Dr. X was sent to Aden. Poor Aden, for not only was the doctor an alcoholic but he was also an extremely bad doctor. I remember meeting a young officer one day, who was bright yellow and told me he felt awful but Dr X could not think what was the matter with him? I suggested he might have jaundice, which was the case!

I was very pleased at the thought of returning to England. Although Sheila and I had had a wonderful time we had been away for nearly five years. We both thought we would join the Wrens. In the meantime I had the opportunity of taking up an invitation to stay with my school friend Rosemary Ogilvie, in New Delhi, where her father was Secretary for Defence in the Indian Government. (He was actually knighted on his retirement.) After the Raid her family had written and warmly asked me for a visit. However, it was far away and the journey expensive. Now all this was altered. When daddy's relief arrived we would all need to travel to Bombay - paid for by the Admiralty - before embarking from there by ship via the Cape for England. So to reach New Delhi I would only have to pay for my return fare between Bombay and Delhi. I raised the money by selling my radio. These were at a premium at this period and I think it is the only time in my life that I have sold anything for double what I bought it for.

10

The Last of the Raj

I left Colombo in October 1942. I was twenty years old. It was an amazing journey, for which these days people pay thousands of pounds to travel on Indian train tours. My family saw me off in Colombo and then I set off for the ferry crossing to Madras in a four-berth sleeping coach, which I had to myself. It was not lonely, as I knew several people on the train and we got out at the various stations and chatted. The trains stopped while we had meals together. The crossing from Ceylon to South India lasted about an hour, as far as I can remember. As we were collecting our luggage to get off the boat and rejoin the train in India, I suddenly realized one of my suitcases had been stolen. Horrified I rushed to the gangway and was just in time to catch the culprit, but it gave me a scare. My two acquaintances were a subaltern and a young married officer's wife. After dinner they evidently went to her compartment for a nightcap and the young man told me next day that she had downed fourteen whiskies and sodas without apparently turning a hair! Next day we arrived at Madras, where a very kind friend of a friend, who entertained me for the day, met me. Then there was another night and a day before I had crossed India to reach Bombay. A circuitous route but, I suppose, in wartime rail routes were a bit odd. Actually it was very beautiful journey. We crossed the Deccan and stopped at tiny villages, where itinerant sellers tried to get me to buy peacock feather fans, and the girls were dressed in the most colourful saris.

In Bombay I spent several days with naval friends who had formerly been in Ceylon, Stephanie and Denis Bingham. Here I went on an orgy of shopping. I had not been in a big town since I left London five years before and though not normally a great shopper, it went to my head on this occasion. From there, there was another twenty four-hour journey to New Delhi. Sir Charles and Rosemary met me at the station and I must have looked very dishevelled but they gave me a great welcome.

It was very interesting coming to India at this moment in history. Independence from British rule was the cry from Ghandi and Nehru but it was to be another four years before this came about. In the meantime I was lucky enough to see a little of the last of the Indian Empire and saw and heard something of how this vast territory was ruled by a handful of Britain's most able sons. Although British members of the Indian Civil Service held practically all the top jobs, they were training Indian juniors to succeed them. These days films and books seem always to portray the few bad administrators that ruled this continent. In fact corruption in the Indian Civil Service was almost unknown, though there was certainly feeling when I was there, among the intelligentsia that the time for Independence had come. The vast majority of the population had experienced a period of peace and prosperity, except for the year of the Mutiny in 1857, that they had never known under their earlier rulers.

Quite young British men were sent to govern enormous tracts of land, to settle disputes, and in some cases temporarily to take over Rajput states during a time of crisis. This had happened to my friend Rosemary's father, Sir Charles Ogilvie. In the 1920s he was ordered to assume charge of the badly run Rajput Nabha State in the United Provinces. The Ogilvies with their two eldest children (George and Rosemary) lived in the palace in great splendour. They owned 6 Rolls Royces, 2 elephants, and a car shaped like a duck. While he was there Sir Charles had the power of life and death over his 'subjects'. How he used this power is testified to by the embellished scroll he was given in an silver case when he left after two years for long leave by his Indian deputy who had helped him:
'When you assumed charge of the State chaos and confusion reigned supreme all round... peace and order had disappeared from the State, and the tension between the two neighbouring Princes had created an atmosphere in which it was well nigh impossible to breathe. In addition the excesses of the Police, on the one hand, and abundance of wild animals that caused heavy ravages on the cattle and the crops of the poor peasants, on the other, had rendered life in both towns and villages miserable and unbearable. Soon after your arrival in the State you set to the hard task of eradicating these evils; evolved order out of chaos; restored peace where there was anarchy; and administered justice to the wronged...

During the history of Nabha State that extends over about 150 years you were the first Englishman to rule over the destinies of its subjects. And it is a matter of supreme gratification to us that we found in you a type of the noblest Englishman that might have set foot in this vast continent. By your sound administration and sympathetic and responsive nature you have not only won our hearts and made yourself popular with even the meanest and the lowest but have also rendered a great and unique service to the British Empire whose distinguished member you are. Your easy acceptability and promptness to afford relief to the aggrieved, and your knowledge of the oriental and vernacular languages which enabled you to converse freely and frequently in the dialect of the masses, and your strict observance of the just and salutary principle 'Nabha for Nabha men' leaves with us an ineffaceable memory and reminds us of our late and revered Chief, Maharajah Hira Singh Sahib Bahadan.'

It was from Sir Charles and the other officials I met that I was able to see something of how this administration worked. Sir Charles and his friend, Gerard Mackworth Young, who had formerly been Head of the British School of Archaeology in Athens, took time to take Rosemary and me around many of the most interesting sights of the seven previous cities of Delhi and to tell me something of how they had governed India.

The Ogilvies had a delightful official bungalow in Hastings Road, New Delhi. When I arrived Lady Ogilvie and Rosemary's younger sisters, Angela and Elizabeth, were still in the hills as the hot weather was not yet over. Rosemary and her father had stayed down, as they were both working. I found the climate delightful, for after the continuous humid hot weather of Ceylon, the high noon temperatures and increasingly cool nights were wonderfully bracing. Indeed, I fear I ate the poor Ogilvies out of house and home! I joined Rosemary working as a volunteer, at the War Department, which was housed in a wing of Viceroy's House. She was on the permanent staff. We cycled to and from the office, as petrol was short in Delhi, unlike Ceylon, where it never seems to have been a problem. Delhi was fairly flat so normally bicycling was not much of a hardship, but I do remember one long ride all uphill, when Gerard Mackworth Young took Rosemary and me up to see the Khutub Minar. This was a vast minaret on the hill above Delhi, about seven miles away. It was worth the journey, as we had a wonderful view and we were able to freewheel home in the cool of the evening.

I played a lot of tennis during the three months I was in Delhi and we went to a great many parties. The city was full of newly arrived American troops and as we girls were at a premium we had a very full social life. Someone gave the US troops a Thanksgiving Party. They had taken great pains to have all the correct dishes, which I listed in a letter back to my family in Trinco. The censor cut out all mention of American troops, which was meant to be secret, but left in details of the food we ate, so it was not very difficult to deduce, for whom the lunch had been intended.

One day I went with Liz the youngest Ogilvie sister, to see the old city of Delhi, with its fabulous fort and Pearl Mosque, and also the fascinating market. This area was really out of bounds, as there had been alarming anti-British riots during the previous summer. However, we went in a tonga (a local horse cart) with a male bearer to guard us and we had no trouble.

On one occasion I was invited with the Ogilvies to a huge ball given in Viceroy's House. We danced on a black and white marble floor. There were mirrors around the walls reflecting the wonderful colours of the Indian ladies' saris, our dresses, as well as the men's brilliant uniforms. War seemed a long way away. Another time we went for a moonlight picnic on one of the Moghul tombs (Humayun's).

While I was staying in Delhi I remembered that the father of another Herons Ghyll school friend, Betty Parsons, was the Police Officer at Agra. They very kindly asked me to stay and I went down there for two or three nights and visited the Taj Mahal. It was not for another forty years that I saw it without scaffolding in all its incomparable beauty. This was partly compensated by the fact that there were no tourists there. The Parsons' house was built in the old style. My bed was in the middle of the room, not

The Taj Mahal

against a wall. This was a precaution against snakes. Also there was no proper bathroom, but a coolie sat outside the bathroom, bringing water, when one wanted a bath, and emptied the lavatory.

Just before Christmas my mother wrote to say that my father's relief had arrived and gave me instructions for my return journey to Bombay, where we were meeting at the Taj Mahal Hotel.

My family had had a wonderful send off from Trinco. During the Raid my father's little motorboat had been sunk. Secretly her crew and other members of father's staff, some of them Tamil craftsmen, had made a beautiful tray from the remains of the copper and white metal fittings from the wreck. It is ornamented with traditional Ceylonese designs of animals, flowers and birds native to the island. This was presented to daddy as a leaving present at the farewell party. It now has a proud place on my mantelpiece. Everyone who worked with my father loved him. I remember once overhearing a signalman grumbling to a mate saying, 'I've just taken a signal to Capt. X. and you'd think I'd sunk the ship it was about, while the Commander always thanks you for everything you do!'

Daddy had completely recovered from his earlier illness and just before I left to go to India, he took part in a Sports' Day's 100 yards race for service men which he won, closely pursued by a sergeant major. I think they both gained a yard for every year's service. As daddy had entered the *Britannia* at fourteen and was then 53, he had quite an advantage.

My family followed the same zigzag route as I had from Colombo to Bombay via Madras. However, they had a strange adventure on the last lap. When they reached the station at Madras, they found that the four-berth compartment had been booked for Commander Harden + two. Few women were travelling at this time. (Indeed, wives had not been able to follow their husbands East since the outset of the war). Thus when my father mother and Sheila arrived at the train they found a young sub-lieutenant occupying the fourth berth. As the journey lasted two nights and a day this was obviously unacceptable. The Station Master hurried up and suggested mummy and Sheila should go in the next carriage - a purdah compartment, (which meant it was reserved for women only). A young Indian girl and an older woman already occupied this. All the windows were tightly closed and the curtains drawn, though they could just see the heavily veiled women in the dark interior. My mother said *sotto voce* to my father, 'I don't mind how many subalterns Sheila and I travel with, but we are not going in that dark, hot compartment.' At this juncture the young officer arrived back from meeting a friend and said he was moving in with him. All seemed to be well. The train left Madras. In the middle of the night the train came to an abrupt halt. The communication cord had been pulled. They seemed to have stopped in a remote place in the Deccan. Eventually officials arrived. Travellers on the linked coach to the purdah compartment had heard shots and when the carriage door was opened the two women had vanished. My mother and Sheila wondered what would have happened if they had been with them? We never heard the outcome as we sailed from India a few days later.

11

Tragedy

We sailed from Bombay just before Christmas 1942 in a passenger ship. There were just a few RAF officers and some troops on board with us. The only excitement I can remember was on Christmas night. Because of the fear of the ship being torpedoed we were not allowed to lock our cabin doors but kept them on a latch. It was a hot night and Sheila was lying in a pale pink chiffon nightie on the lower bunk. Suddenly we heard raucous laughter outside our cabin. We realized it was some of the men obviously having had a good party, returning to their quarters. Next moment our door was flung open and several men gazed in. One of them saw Sheila and cried out, 'You're my ideal!' Sheila normally so gentle and slight, leapt from her bunk, seized a solid torch and struck the intruder through the half-open door. She must have hit him quite hard on the shoulder. He let out an oath and by this time I had joined Sheila and we managed to slam and bolt the door, as we yelled for daddy who was in the communicating cabin. He rushed out into the corridor and there was a short fight in the companionway! At that moment a duty officer must have appeared and the men were taken away. The next day they were charged with striking an officer and I suppose for attempted attack on us. However, daddy did not press the charge as it was Christmas!

During the latter part of the voyage father became very ill with a high fever, so that when we arrived at Durban he was immediately given sick leave. The South Africans were immensely hospitable and had a scheme for entertaining visiting service personnel. So we went up to stay on a beautiful farm near Kokstad in East Griqualand, in the very north of the Cape Province. It was right in the mountains with a river running in a loop through the property. It was great fun, for when we went swimming one could sit in a tyre at the top and then were whooshed down to the bottom, where you got out and started again. There were also lovely walks. Sheila and I borrowed ponies and rode, while mummy and daddy went on foot. As our mounts were so slow or maybe we did not manage them very well, Sheila and I always seemed to arrive later than our parents. After a couple of weeks, daddy recovered and during the last days of his leave we took the opportunity of going by train to the Kruger Game Reserve in the Transvaal via the Drakensberg Mountains.

As it was wartime and also the wrong season, much of the reserve was closed. This meant that we had the vast area of the Park practically to ourselves. Daddy had hired a car with a driver and we were just looking at some giraffes, (one was not allowed to get out,) when we saw another car approaching. It turned out to be the game warden's wife. When she saw that daddy was in uniform she immediately invited us all over to the main (unopened) section of the Reserve on the next day, when she said that she would take and show us more animals. It was a wonderful opportunity. Their camp was all enclosed against the animals in wire fencing. She told us that when she had taken her children to the London zoo they had been amazed to find that the animals were behind wires! She drove us down to a small river and said that we could get out, as there were no other visitors, and we might see some crocodiles. She went on ahead with daddy, attired in a khaki skirt and puttees, with a knife stuck in her belt, while we followed slightly behind. We did notice some pad marks in the sand, but thought nothing of it. We did notice however that our driver had stayed behind in the Land Rover. Afterwards we asked him why he had not come to see the crocodiles. 'Well' he said, 'I saw the prints of simba (lions) and thought if you were all attacked I would blow the horn!' We felt it would have been a bit late by then!

Daddy had now quite recovered, we returned to Durban to find out about our onward passage to the UK. To our great dismay we discovered that only daddy was to continue. The submarine attacks were at their height and it was considered too dangerous to send all the women and children who were at this time, waiting for ships to sail to England without a strong convoy. Also after our recent victories in North Africa, a great many Italian prisoners-of-war needed to be transported to America.

While daddy was waiting for his passage we went to a farm near Pietermaritzburg. It was hilly country and also our hostess was a keen tennis player, so we had a pleasant time. One day we were told there was to be a Zulu wedding in the 'native' reserve, which bordered the farm. It was quite a long walk, taking about two or three hours, but it was well worthwhile when we got there. There were several little *rondavels* (little wooden huts) and all the girls dressed in colourful cotton sari-type dresses began dancing with the bride, the farewell to her youth. (She was only about sixteen!) Then we saw on the surrounding hills, young men with spears approaching, circling round. They got nearer and nearer, then the bridegroom seized his bride and bore her off! They must have carried on with festivities well into the night, but we began our trek back to the farm slightly impeded by a horrendous thunderstorm, which mother hated.

After a week or so the time came to go back to Durban for daddy to join his ship the *Empress of Canada* for his journey on to England. He sailed on the 1st of March and the three of us returned to the farm outside Maritzburg (Pietermaritzburg). On the 14th Sheila was in the sitting room when she heard an announcement by Lord Haw Haw (the traitorous British broadcaster widely used by the Nazis) saying that a U-boat had sunk the *Empress of Canada* on the 13th. Devastated she rushed to me and we discussed what we should do? Many of these reports were inaccurate and were just used for propaganda purposes. We decided that we would wait to tell mummy until we had found out what had really happened. We went to the very nice farmer's wife and she said that she would drive down to Durban next day and go to the Naval Office to discover the full information. It was some of the worst few days of my life. She came back to say that the ship had been torpedoed, but a great many of the passengers and crew had been saved, as the ship had gone down not too far from Freetown. We still said nothing to mummy. That day while we were having lunch, her wedding ring fell off. She had never taken it off since she was married at Radlett so many years before.

A few days later a naval chaplain came to the farm and broke the news that daddy had not been among the rescued. Although he was only taking passage in the ship, he was the senior officer on board and being him, had stayed to the last to organize the escape of the Italian prisoners and as many as possible of everyone else before the ship went down. In the First World War he had won the DSO for rescuing his fellow shipmates, while in the Second he died saving his enemies. A few weeks later Brodles (Admiral Brodie) wrote the following letter to *The Times:*

'I learned that Commander George Harden, DSO, RN, lost his life through remaining in a torpedoed ship to help get out rafts. Past 50, a sick man, and a passenger, he might indeed ought to have gone with the rest to the boats. To tackle the nearest job, without fuss or thought for himself is what is what one expected from "Jo". His quiet devotion whether to the Navy, which gave him slight recognition, or to his family, who gave him full measure, was natural to him. His brains and industry at any but the Navy's leanest period for promotion would have taken him far, but his modesty probably tipped the scales against him. During the 1914-18 war Harden won the DSO by handling his ship in the Tigris with seamanship and determination under a murderous fire. Since that war I saw more of him on skis than in ships. It was "Jo" who worked out the duller details of an expedition, grinned if a daughter made rings round him, helped neatly and skillfully anyone in any sort of trouble, and who assured me that carrying an extra pack helped his balance going uphill. Carrying others' packs uphill was his way. The Navy has more of his sort, but for the rest of the "Four-in-hand" his loss must indeed be irreparable. Their many friends made in Africa, Austria, or Ceylon, can only share with them a heartening, happy, and proud memory.'

My father, Commander G.E.Harden, DSO, RN

Later we heard that a cove, a buoy and a point had been named Harden in Trincomalee Harbour as a tribute to my father.

12

Returning to England

My mother, Sheila and I were now stuck in South Africa. It was at this devastating moment, that the kind Sparling relations, whom we had stayed with so often on their tea estate Mooloya, in Ceylon, but who had been evacuated with their young son after the Raid, arrived at the farm. They had bought a house near Maritzburg and invited us to come and stay until we got a passage home. It was a lovely villa in the hills above the town, but we were so miserable and longing to return home, that we could not enjoy the beautiful scenery and walks. Of course we still held a tiny hope that daddy might have been picked up by a passing ship, though I do not think any of the three of us held out any real hope. About a fortnight later we went back to Durban to find out if there was any more news of the sinking and also if there was any prospect of a ship to England. To our astonishment mother was told that if we could be at Durban Station in two hours' time, we could board a troop train leaving for Cape Town and a heavily convoyed ship bound for England. We rushed back to the hotel and collected our luggage. We had been away for five years and had fifteen cases of luggage between us when we joined the train with about 5,000 other women and children who had been waiting passage. There was another woman already in our compartment and so when a porter flung in more luggage, thinking it was a four-berth coach, we threw it out again. Then its owner appeared for it was a six-berth compartment. This was Angela Sarell, who remained one of our dearest friends, and indeed during this sad journey, it made all the difference having her with us.

The train journey to Cape Town lasted thirty-six hours and we travelled through some beautiful country, including vineyards. These were thick with ripe, delicious eating grapes, which we bought at one of the stations. They were particularly welcome as all food had run out and only the children were allowed anything to eat. On arrival at Cape Town we were met by a group of ladies with trestle tables set out with food. It was most welcome. The only time in my life I have been fed by volunteers. The *Britannic* was lying in the harbour and we were efficiently taken on board and allotted cabins. Ours was way below the water line and had been turned from a single berth to a three-berth cabin. It was so small that you had to throw yourself in sideways to get to bed. I imagine it was rather like the Japanese hostels one reads about now! Sheila was always a bit claustrophobic after this voyage. It was the worst period of the U-boat war, but we had the *Warspite* and a number of other warships guarding us and I do not think we ran into any real danger until we neared the UK. Those last few days were dangerous and we had to sleep in our clothes. We stopped at Freetown and mother went on shore to see if there was any news of survivors from the *Empress of Canada* but there were none. We sailed on and ran into a severe storm off Ireland. As I have always been an excellent sailor, I went on deck and have never seen such waves. They reached to the bridge of the *Warspite* and the little destroyers completely disappeared under them. However, they probably saved us for U-boats, at that period, could not operate in heavy seas. Submarines must have been around, as I remember seeing depth charges being dropped.

We sighted the coast of Ireland at the beginning of May and there was snow on the mountains. We steamed into Liverpool on the 13th. We all knew that food was very short in England and so were glad to be handed out sandwiches for our onward journey. The first thing we had to do on landing was to collect our luggage. As manpower was scarce all our cases were dumped in a huge warehouse near the ship in alphabetical order. Thus a vast mound of 'Hs' greeted us to sort through. As there were some five or six thousand people in our ship, it was a ghastly and very difficult task to find our fifteen trunks and suitcases. Once we had somehow piled them together we had to telephone my godmother Di Thursby, who lived in the Cotswolds near Stow-on-the-Wold and ask her if she could take us in until we had found somewhere to go.

No one knew we had left South Africa, because security did not allow any messages to be sent. Sheila and I found a call box and I put through a phone call to Stow, as I knew Di worked at the Food Office. Of course I had no idea of the number to ring and I also had trouble with the coins. We had been out of England for five years and all the coinage was strange. Eventually I got through to the Post Office in Stow and asked for the Food Office, only to be told that it was in Moreton-in-the-Marsh. However, the kind operator transferred me, as I fumbled for more unfamiliar coins. Here I actually contacted Di. She was an angel. She leapt on her bicycle and rode the four miles back to her pretty little thatched house in Broadwell and prepared rooms for her unexpected guests. We somehow managed to get a naval driver to take us to the nearest station.

The trip from Liverpool to Stow necessitated five changes. Not an easy undertaking with fifteen pieces of luggage. However what I remember of the journey was the beauty of England in the early summer. After five years in the East to see all the blossoms out and the wild flowers among the green of the fields was wonderful. We had heard so much of England at war that we had forgotten how much of tranquillity remained. I could hardly believe how rosy cheeked and well all the children looked and when we took out our sandwiches, everyone else did the same and we realized that things might be difficult but starvation was a long way away. It may sound trite but the old song 'There'll always be an England and England shall be free.' came into my mind.

13

The War in England

We had arrived. It was summer, so the clothes we had with us were adequate for the moment but we had very little else. Much of the furniture that we had had in Ceylon had been lost at sea. All our silver and carpets had been sunk. The goods that had been stored in London had been bombed. My mother's income was a very small war widow's pension and a few dividends. We had no house and for the next few weeks no jobs. Luckily what we had were wonderful friends. Di Thursby opened her house to us in the lovely Cotswolds, the Colvin's stored the little furniture, including a 17th century Dutch chest with a rat inside it, which was rescued from a stricken ship coming back from Ceylon, and naval friends rallied round us and helped in every sort of way.

Mother was devastated by daddy's death but was wonderfully brave. Hers was a sterling character. Not conventionally beautiful, she was very attractive with dark hair and blue eyes, a legacy from her Celtic forbears, and she had immense charm. She was one of the most optimistic people I have ever known. Whenever one arrived for a visit, she would always say, ' What a wonderful time to arrive!'. Perhaps it was just teatime, or there would be time to unpack before dinner. She had a very strong religious faith and I think this sustained her a great deal during this sad time. Now she had to reorganize her life and she did this with great courage. After her death in 1981 a young friend wrote, 'Everyone loved her!'

First we had to find war work. Sheila and I decided that we would ask permission to serve in the Admiralty, rather than enter the Wrens, as we thought mummy would be so lonely if we were sent off to some distant station. We therefore all presented ourselves for an interview in Whitehall. Mummy and I had no qualifications, though I had been a cipher officer in Trinco. This did not seem to count as I was entered as a clerk grade 3 (at about £3 a week); I imagine the lowest Civil Service position, as was mother, while Sheila with her Sorbonne degree, was rated as a signals officer. Mother and I had to take a simple literacy test and were then assigned to the Citadel. This is the ivy covered building next to the Admiralty made of such dense concrete that it is now impossible to destroy, as its demolition would also blow up the entire neighbourhood. Sheila was sent there too. All our offices were very near each other. I was assigned to the Meteorological Department and was interviewed by a pleasant naval captain (Met.) He began by saying, 'I expect you are an excellent mathematician?' I had to disillusion him about this. Daddy had tried to teach Sheila and me simple arithmetic when we lived in Austria, but though he had been an excellent mathematician himself, he had no idea how to teach the subject, and as neither of us had any aptitude or interest in it, we merely scraped through our School Certificates. I was now instructed in plotting the weather maps, while in nearby offices mother decoded the top-secret messages of Winston Churchill, and Sheila dealt with the signals. The Citadel was an interesting place to be, as it was from here that the admirals and captains directed the naval war. It was July 1943 and plans were already afoot for the Second Front.

The Citadel and the old Admiralty building
(Courtesy Christine Ottewill)

But to return to more basic things, where were we going to live? Mummy phoned a cousin Joan Andrews, who had moved into the then ultra modern block of flats Dolphin Square, in 1938. It remained the largest block of flats in Europe until quite recently. I remember that granny had written out to us in Ceylon describing a visit she had paid to Joan just before the war and giving us a description of the Square: its swimming pool, squash courts, tennis court, shops, and underground garage. Now Joan spoke to the Manager and told him of our plight and we found ourselves ensconced in No 410 Rodney House, Dolphin Square, just before my 21st birthday. I have lived there ever since! (Though we moved to an unfurnished flat in 1947.)

The next problem was that none of the three of us knew how to cook, not even an egg. In fact, mother told me later that when she was shown the kitchen in our new flat, she thought, 'That's one room I'll never use!' She was soon disillusioned. Joan taught us elementary things like fish-pies and with the help of recipe books we soon became quite proficient. Although food was short in wartime England and excessively dull, I was never hungry. Lord Woolton did a marvellous job with the food rationing and there was almost no black marketeering.

However, one could play around with rations. For instance we did not like cheese, so swapped our cheese coupons for eggs from the Knoxes, friends who lived in the country and had chickens. John was a naval captain and I remember that when he came to dinner one night two eggs had broken in his smart uniform jacket pocket! The things I really missed were butter and sweets. Coffee was never rationed as it was not drunk nearly as much then as it is now, and it was felt that if people were given coupons for it, they would feel they had to take them and then there would not be enough to go round. Cooking one learned by trial and error. I remember one night coming in to find Sheila had made what smelled like a delicious savoury rice dish, but she had not realized that you needed to cook the rice before frying it.

Our flat in Dolphin Square was furnished, with maid service. Our maid was called Florence and had begun life with an aristocratic family in the country. She told us marvellous 'Upstairs, Downstairs' tales of what life was like in a great household between the wars. They worked very hard, but etiquette was even stricter below than above stairs and the butler, housekeeper, and ladies' maids had their own little rooms, where the lowlier servants served them in great style. I think, when their betters had departed, the underlings then had great times in the servants' hall.

By the summer of 1943 the worst of the German bombing raids were over, until the advent of the V 1s and V 2s in 1944. However, there were raids about once a week. Joan had a little enclosed box-room on the first floor. We were on the fourth and she had a flat on the third. She very unselfishly insisted that mummy should sleep in her box-room on a camp bed if a raid became bad, while she Sheila and I fixed up mattresses outside in the enclosed corridors, where we slept if it became too noisy. We usually began the night in our beds and then went down if it seemed dangerous. Dolphin Square had been hit several times before we came home but luckily, it was not touched during the second half of the war, though neighbouring buildings were damaged. Other people also slept in the corridor and I remember one couple brought down an enormous double mattress, with all its sheets and pillows and the wife slept with her mink coat folded beside her!

Once after a bad raid when many buildings were alight when we went back to bed we found that all the incidents had been dealt with by next morning. Very different from the Raid in Trinco, when all the workers had fled and nothing was cleared up for weeks. That morning when I was driving in the 24 bus to work down Whitehall, I thought how extraordinary that there seemed no sign of damage, only to be confronted by half the Treasury building lying across the road near the Cenotaph.

We worked long hours at the Admiralty - a fourteen hour night and a ten hour day-which allowed one to travel most of the year in daylight. The long night watches exempted us from fire-fighting duties. As we lived in central London the 24 buses carried us to and from Whitehall fairly efficiently. At that time there was also the 134 bus which actually started at Dolphin Square. Once inside the Admiralty one entered by tortuous underground passages until one reached the Citadel. It was far below street level so even if there were raids outside, one could hear nothing. We were allowed time off for meals in the rather squalid canteen, but in the daytime we usually went across to the National Gallery. Here there was an excellent canteen run by several ladies, headed by Lady Fremantle. She most kindly supplemented the rations allowed her, with vegetables from her country garden and by her imaginative dishes called 'Woolton Pie' or some such names! There were also for the musical, excellent concerts.

During the night we were allowed to sleep for a couple of hours in makeshift dormitories. One night I happened to be alone in this room and got maddened by the clock, which ticked every half-minute. I kept adding up the minutes' rest I still had. The clock so got on my nerves that I climbed out of my bunk and had a look at it. It just seemed fixed to the wall by an ordinary plug. I pulled this out and the clock promptly stopped. Very pleased with my cleverness, I climbed back into my berth and immediately fell asleep. An hour or so later, the dormitory having been by then filled up with other office girls, the door was flung open by two infuriated electricians. 'Here it is!' they said, gazing at the dangling cord I had pulled out. 'Who did this?' 'I'm afraid it was me', I owned up. 'Do you realize you have stopped every clock in the Admiralty?' Luckily they could not execute me and after all we won the war!

Between plotting the weather maps there were quite long intervals when there was nothing to do, and during this time I began to write a book on Queen Elizabeth of York, the mother of Henry VIII. I did most of the writing at home, but I would type out the manuscript in the office, and would go and do some research around London during my time off. It was a pleasant antidote to war to look into the past and was eventually to help me gain a place in London University.

We entertained a good bit during these years, just having friends around to share our sparse meals and we also went down to the country when we had leave. By 1944 we all realized that the Second Front was imminent. I guessed where the landing was to be by the number of forecasts for the Normandy beaches and also by the worried admirals, who kept coming in to the office and gazing at the weather maps. I realized later how vital the weather forecasts had been to the success of Operation Overlord. There had been such a spate of bad weather just before this date that the Germans did not think a cross-Channel operation would be possible. However, our Met. Officers forecast a short respite on 6-7th June, which just allowed the huge fleets to cross.

I heard details of the invasion fleet quite recently, from one of my cousins Jack Oldfield, who was in HMS *Magpie* when she led and escorted the very first of the sixty groups of Force G bound for the beaches at Arromanches in Normandy. Their job was to sail until they had reached the spot where the small craft could land the troops for the assault on the beaches. He told me that as they got nearer and nearer they could not believe that the enemy would not engage them. But though the German batteries did not open fire on their ships, to quote from Jack's memoirs 'the euphoria was short lived. Those to whom we had just waved and wished good luck, discharged at the water's edge, were now scrambling across the sandy beach. But the beach had been mined. We on the bridge could see through our glasses all too clearly what was happening. It was a slaughter. The beach was littered with our men's bodies some writhing in pain, others lying quietly in death. We doubted that any had survived...to the planners...1 number 1 group had done its job successfully - we had cleared the beaches for groups 2 to 60. Looking at the scene I thought here lie the victims, the burnt offering demanded by the gods of war. I prayed silently to God in the familiar words, "eternal rest grant to them Lord, and may light perpetual shine upon them." Jack said that this leading of the vast armada to France was probably the most extraordinary event in his long and eventful life. (He lived until he was one hundred).

While Jack was fighting at sea his eighty-three year old Aunt Maud had successfully fought another battle, which had preserved his property! Earlier in the war when the German invasion was daily expected, it was decided to evacuate the civilian population from the southern coastal regions. Doddington Place, Jack's estate, is situated a few miles inland from Dover the likely landing area. Aunt Maud and her elderly maid living in a few rooms of the large Victorian house, were visited one day by a young subaltern, who explained that civilians were being evacuated from this area for their protection and that Doddington Place was to be requisitioned as an army headquarters. Aunt Maud the formidable widow of General Jefferies (a descendant of the notorious judge of that name), politely replied that she quite understood that the army might need the house, but that she and her maid would be quite satisfied with a few of the many rooms. 'But Madam' stammered the lieutenant, 'you would not be safe here. The Germans do terrible things.' 'Do you mean young man,' retorted Aunt Maud, that I and my maid both over eighty are afraid of being raped? No we are staying here. I'm too old to be hustled away.' Next day the colonel arrived at Doddington. 'You do realize Mrs Jefferies what worries you would have if you stayed here and all the bad language you would hear?' 'Do you not realize Colonel that the wife of a general during all the years I was with him when he served in the army, has not heard every swear word in the English language?' Aunt Maud retorted. She remained at Doddington Place throughout the war. Every day she walked with her stick, chatting to the men and making friends with the two individuals she considered most important - the Colonel and the Sergeant Major - with the result that not a picture in the house nor a flower in the garden was vandalized. Jack returned at the end of the war to find his heritage perfectly preserved.

To return to Operation Overlord, as the invasion of Europe was code-named. Sheila and mummy knew everything from all the signals that had passed through their hands, but we never discussed our work. On 6th June mother and I happened to be in a jeweller's shop Carringtons in the West End, when the assistant told us that the invasion had started. Two days later I was on night watch, when Sheila phoned me to say that there was a strange raid going on, not like any that we had had before. The aeroplanes seemed to have flames coming out of them then the engines stopped, and after a pause they exploded. That was the beginning of the attack of the notorious V 1s. The date was 8th June.

The V 1 was a jet-propelled pilotless aircraft twenty-five feet long, costing only £125 and with a range of 200-250 miles. 10,492 were aimed at London but luckily only 2,419 reached the capital. In the first two weeks V 1s killed 1,600 people, seriously injured another 4,500, and damaged 200,000 houses; the casualty rate in June 1944 was as heavy as it had been in September 1940. It was only fortunate that Hitler failed to use this new weapon earlier.

Everyone began talking about these strange new bombers now called Flying Bombs. They began to reach London thick and fast. One would see this elongated object with flames seemingly coming from its tail making a peculiar humming drone. Then suddenly the noise would stop and the bomb would dive to earth and explode causing great damage. If the noise continued you were safe, but once it stopped you knew it would explode a mile or two beyond. A black signal was put up somewhere between Dolphin Square and Westminster Cathedral when the bombs - soon nicknamed doodlebugs - were in our vicinity. We had friends near the Cathedral and if one came down near us they would say, ' Poor Hardens I hope they are all right.' and similarly if a flying bomb passed over us towards Victoria, we would say 'I hope the Mackenzies are OK.'

At work in the Citadel one was unaware of any bombing but naturally we were worried about each other, as we were not necessarily all on watch at the same time.

The day after the first V 1 came over, I went down to spend my day off with friends near Reigate. At first the Germans did not get the range of London and many doodlebugs exploded around their country house, while we took shelter in their cellar. Actually the outer southern suburbs were very badly hit. One V 1 in Bromley killed the fiancé of one of my colleagues, I sadly remember.

During the night I was often sent across to the old Admiralty building to deliver weather reports to the various captain and officials. Because of the blackout restrictions it was very badly illuminated and it was quite eerie walking down the long corridors passing statues of long dead admirals. One year we spent Christmas Eve night at the Admiralty and during our break we went across Trafalgar Square to Midnight Mass at St Martin's-in-the-Fields. The church was crammed and there was a wonderful atmosphere. I think it was the first time I had been to a midnight service. They were not at all usual in the Church of England at that time. Before the war the usual Anglican services were the 8 o'clock Communion, followed at 11 by Matins or Evensong at 6. The present Parish Communion at 9.30 or 10 a.m. only became the norm during the fifties.

One of our constant visitors and friend during this period was (Commander) Harry Mackenzie, a contemporary of daddy's on the *Britannia*. Between the wars he had been head of the British War Graves commission in Northern France and he and his wife lived in a beautiful sixteenth-century house in Arras. Like many Scots he was rather fey (visionary) and he had had a strong premonition of the coming war. Also he once told me that he had seen daddy smiling at him, while he was working in the Admiralty, as if asking him to keep an eye on us. Earlier during the main Blitz he had been quietly reading a newspaper in his nearby club - the United Services Club - when a bomb exploded outside and a fragment came sideways through the window and took off one of his toes. He was then carried on a stretcher, to the First Aid Room for treatment through the underground passages of the Admiralty, where all the secretaries, etc. were taking cover and who made commiseratory remarks as he passed. He made a great joke about it, though it must have been very painful.

Naturally the bombing was frightening, but you did get fairly immune to fear. For instance I remember that mother asked Lucy Brode, who lived near Midhurst, whether she would like to come up for lunch. Lucy replied on the telephone quite seriously, that she would only like to come if mummy could be certain that there would be no bombing? As my mother was not in the Führer's confidence she could not reassure her!

We were at a matinee of a Shakespeare play in Regent's Park when the first V 2 exploded. I had no knowledge of this new device, Hitler's next secret weapon, though mother and Sheila had seen signals predicting their use. It was the 8th September. The V 2 was a rocket 50 feet long and 6 feet in circumference. It could reach a speed of 3,600 m.p.h. It was impossible to intercept and arrived without any warning. Luckily for us our armies were approaching the V 2 firing sites when they were launched, and London only received some 517 rockets and other parts of England 537. As one never heard them coming I never found them very frightening. One would either be dead or alive so it was not worth worrying! The Germans then turned this weapon on poor Antwerp, which had even heavier casualties than those in England.

At this time we saw our cousin Dick Harden again. He was now one of General Montgomery's liaison officers. He had fought with him from El Alamein through Normandy to Berlin. He had had many adventures; the most unusual was in February 1945. He and another liaison officer Carol Mather, were ordered to fly in a light Auster aircraft to a rendezvous just behind the forward line in France. Flying at 1,000 feet, they were intercepted by a Focke-Wulf 190. Ground fire drove the fighter off, but to Dick's horror he realized that their pilot had been killed and Mather badly wounded. Dick had never flown before, but he managed to take the controls and crash-landed the plane into a swamp.

In June he arrived at our flat and asked if he could sleep on our floor. (We had no spare room.) He had brought the terms of the German surrender from General Montgomery for the King and Churchill to sign. He told us that evening that Churchill had kept insisting that it should be 'unconditional surrender'. The German generals naturally insisted that this should be spelled out. After all unconditional surrender could mean that every German was to be slaughtered. Finally it was all written down. In fact the German civilian population as well as their army fled to the

West, much preferring to be under British and American troops than the vengeful Soviet hordes.

We heard some years later that the Hungarian friends Dinko and Kitty de Balla, who had driven us to Budapest in 1935, had been in that city when the Russian's sacked it in 1945. Dinko hid Kitty in their bathroom, as the Russian soldiers went through all the blocks of flats raping the women systematically floor by floor. He just found himself praying, 'Jesus! Jesus!' Suddenly, at the storey below, the soldiers desisted and went back to their barracks. Soon after Dinko and Kitty managed to reach the United States embassy. She was an American citizen and they were flown to the States.

War ended abruptly with the dropping of the atom bombs on Hiroshima and Nagasaki. Now we only tend to think of these events as horrific and perhaps, unnecessary. But that was not how we received the news in 1945. Our feelings were unbelievable relief that the war was over and that all the slaughter would stop. Our horror against the Japanese was exasperated by the terrible pictures of the pathetic ex-prisoners-of-war returning from their Far East enslavement. I was talking to an American neighbour a few years ago. He told me that he was in army draft training for the invasion of Japan. Their sergeant warned them that their life expectancy on landing would be three minutes. This loss of life would no doubt, have been as great, or greater among the Japanese. So the dreadful price of the dropping of the atom bombs not only ended the war but also, prevented casualties in all the armies.

14

Post-War Years

With the war ended what were Sheila and I going to do? Sheila luckily had her Sorbonne degree and through a friend of a friend, obtained an interview with Sir Paul Butler. Sir Paul had been Consul General before the war in Tokyo and spoke and wrote perfect Japanese. He had been asked by Chatham House (The Royal Institute of International Affairs) to write a book on Japan, showing how that country had become increasingly determined to fight the West. He now needed an assistant. His daughter Joan told me the other day how delighted her father had been when Sheila joined him. He predicted a great future for her, as she was so intelligent as well as being so pretty and charming. Although we had lived four years in Ceylon, Sheila at that time had not travelled further east as the war was raging, so she began steeping herself in histories of the Far East. She soon began writing some of the chapters for Sir Paul. (Later she travelled all over these countries and became something of an authority on them.) Chatham House had commissioned the book called *Japanese Behaviour in War and Conquest*, but Sir Paul told Sheila just as it was completed, that as the American foundation was sponsoring it they had been advised that US government policy had changed towards Japan, which they now wanted to conciliate. According to Sir Paul, they influenced Chatham House to renege on his contract. All his years of research and writing went for nothing.

While Sheila began working for Sir Paul, Angela Sarrell (later Cruickshank) suggested that I should apply for a place at London University. I longed to do this but difficulties seemed almost insurmountable. Perhaps due to my haphazard education, I only had a meagre 5 credits in my School Certificate not including Latin, which was compulsory for a History degree, nor had I any 'A' levels. Apart from these obstacles, all the college entrance exams had been held and the places filled the previous October! But I now discovered that because of the war, those would-be students whose education had been broken because of this, were allowed entry at the equivalent of GSCE credits for matriculation, provided they passed four 'A' levels after their first year. One just had to take an entrance paper for one's chosen college and a paper in my case, on history. I also had to gain a credit in Latin. I wrote around to the various colleges in London, asking if they would have a place for me. Westfield College, in Hampstead (now absorbed into Queen Mary College) had as its Principal Lady Stocks, who interviewed me and agreed to my coming as a day student, provided I passed the Latin exam. I learned many years later that my acceptance by Westfield was due to the fact that I had written and researched my book on Elizabeth of York. I gained distinctions in Latin, easy enough with a good crammer. I had to read it up to my finals, but I can now hardly translate a tombstone!

In February 1946 I went with Angela to Jersey. The island so recently under German occupation, was not yet open for ordinary tourists. However, Angela's grandmother had been immured there throughout the war and she was given a pass, with one for me to visit her. (The old lady had survived quite well.) We stayed at a guest-house in St. Helier and went for long walks exploring the lovely island, without any other visitors to clutter the beauty spots. The residents in the hotel - all islanders - much enjoyed seeing visitors from the mainland and telling us stories of their wartime experiences. On the whole we gathered that the Germans had behaved quite correctly. Perhaps, because unlike the inhabitants of their European occupied territories, Great Britain had never given in. During the last winter the islanders said that the German troops were starving and were reduced to eating root vegetables from the fields. While the rest of Europe was conquered, the Channel Islands to avoid casualties, were not freed until after peace was signed. Angela and I flew back after our holiday. It was the first time I had been in an aeroplane - a bi-plane.

In October 1946 I arrived at Westfield College, Hampstead Heath for my first term at university. I was twenty-four years old. However, I was not alone in being so much older than is usual for undergraduates. About one third of that year's intake across the country, had fought in the war or done war work, so their educations had been interrupted. I now had to take four subjects in my first year as well as doing my history

Honour's work. Apart from history, I studied English Literature, Ancient History, and the compulsory Latin during my first year. They were all subjects that I enjoyed except perhaps the Latin, so it was no hardship though reducing my Honour's time to two rather than three years, probably was a handicap.

My first day was rather alarming. I stood disconsolately by the notice-board at lunch time not knowing anybody, when a girl came up to me and asked if I was a 'fresher?'-the name for newcomers. 'Why don't you come along to my room and meet my friends?' she said. It was so kind. Westfield was at that time a residential college for women and I was one of the very few who was not boarding, so I had no study to work in. Now my new friends generously invited me to use their rooms, when I was at college during the day and in return, I was able to ask them back to our flat in Dolphin Square for meals sometimes.

I spent a very happy three years at Westfield. I took part in many games particularly tennis and squash, playing in the University teams and captaining the tennis team at Westfield, when we won the National Union of Students tennis championship in 1949. I also captained a Trans-Atlantic quiz between Westfield and an American College on the BBC. I am glad to say we won by a whisker!

I found to my delight that I was eligible for a grant for my tuition and living expenses as my mother, on a tiny war widows' pension and few dividends, had very little spare cash. I think students these days spend much more money than we did. For instance I never went out to pubs, nor did any of my colleagues, or meals except very occasionally, nor did I smoke. This was not noble; as after I had tried a cigarette at sixteen, I thought it was so disgusting that I have never put one in my mouth again. It was not necessary to buy many books except for those required. One could use Westfield's excellent library.

As I was specializing in Renaissance Italy I was sent on a course during one of the summer vacations, to Jesus College, Cambridge. It was a wonderful fortnight. We had digs in the town, but spent the day in the college listening to lectures morning and evening, while the rest of the days were free to be punted down the Cam by boy friends or in playing tennis. One day Dorothy Sayers, who had just completed her translation of *The Divine Comedy*, lectured us. The then Italian ambassador to St. James had been invited down to give the address of thanks. However, it was really very amusing. He had obviously disagreed with every word Dorothy Sayers had uttered. After very perfunctory thanks, he pulled from his breast pocket a well-worn copy of *La Divina Commedia* and bursting into Italian, proceeded to give his own interpretation of his country's classic. Unfortunately for his cause, few of us could understand his erudite Italian and his peroration was lost on us!

The immediate post-war years were very stark. Food shortages were strangely enough, worse than during the war. I imagine that due to a more generous attitude by the victors than following the 1914-18 war, quite rightly the first priority was to feed the starving victims of Hitler's tyranny. This was the first time whale meat was imposed upon us. It was the most disgusting food that one could think of - a horrible mixture of fish and awful meat. This period also happened to coincide with an extraordinarily severe winter. Luckily, in Dolphin Square the heating always worked fairly efficiently, but friends' houses were torture in cold weather.

However, we still managed to have a great deal of fun and social life, and balls started again. I was even presented at Court - to King George VI and Queen Elizabeth - though these presentations had now been reduced to Royal Garden parties. Social presentations were abolished soon after, except for those who had earned them, after obtaining an Honour or for excellent public service. My presentation was quite undeserved, but I enjoyed the occasion!

In 1947 after a long wait we were able to move into an unfurnished flat in Dolphin Square. The one we took - No 603 Raleigh House - my present home, on the sixth floor overlooking the Thames, had just been relinquished by General de Gaulle and the Free French. In later years we met a French count, who had lived there in the war and remembered Dolphin Square with much affection.

While I had been at Westfield Sheila had been gaining experience in foreign affairs. After Sir Paul left she then worked for Shane Olver and finally Peter Calvocoressi, helping them to *write The Annual Surveys of International Affairs*.

When I graduated in 1949 I too went to Chatham House, working in the Press Library on Germany and the War Crimes sections. Even reading these horrific accounts of Nazi atrocities nearly made me physically sick. While I was at Westfield I had kept very quiet about my knowledge of German, as I foresaw that I would be given endless German tomes to digest if my tutor Nicolai Rubenstein, knew that I could read the language. He has remained a lifelong friend and I have recently confessed!

15

The Oxford University Press

I was made redundant by Chatham House after only nine months as their money was running out. In the end it proved fortunate, for Nicolai was a room-mate of an editor at the London office of the Oxford University Press, who told him that their librarian was leaving and I should apply for the job.

I had been out of work for some months and was feeling very despondent. It is horrible to think that nobody wants your services. I went to be interviewed by the then publisher, Mr Geoffrey Cumberlege in great trepidation. He asked me about my previous work and was surprisingly, pleased that I had had endless experience answering telephones, when I had been in the Meteorological Office during the war (I did soon realize that answering the phone was an integral part of my work). He then wanted to know where I had been school? I answered, 'A small school called, Herons Ghyll, but I don't expect you will ever have heard of it?' 'Not at all' he replied with a happy smile, 'when it was a private house I went to a ball there and met my dear wife!' I got the job and spent the next thirty years as London librarian of the Oxford University Press.

The Oxford University Press is the largest (certainly at this time) and oldest non-governmental printing press in the world. Theodoric Rood set up a printing press in 1478 in Oxford - only two years after Caxton had opened the first printing press in England in 1476. It has continued almost uninterruptedly ever since. In the Civil War when Charles 1 had his Court in Oxford, it published many of the propaganda leaflets issued by the Royalists. Once I went down to the old warehouse on the Banbury road, when I was looking for some records for an exhibition I was organizing on the history of the Press. Climbing up a rickety ladder, I found some of these pamphlets untidily stacked on a top shelf and evidently long forgotten. Since then I imagine they have been carefully catalogued.

When I joined the OUP (as it was always called) in 1951 it was divided into two main sections. The Oxford Office - called the Clarendon Press, where the most scholarly works are published, and the London Office. (The Departments that had been in London were moved to Oxford in the early eighties.) I should explain that the OUP is a department of the University of Oxford and is ruled by the Secretary to the Delegates. The Delegates a body of academics chosen from among the most distinguished Oxford dons, are responsible for the highly academic books, bearing the coveted imprint 'at the Clarendon Press'.

During the late nineteenth century it was realized that it would be useful indeed essential, to have a London outlet for selling Oxford books. A London publisher was appointed - first Henry Frowde, then Sir Humphrey Milford - followed in my time by Mr. Geoffrey Cumberlege and lastly Sir John Brown. The London office quickly expanded for after all, London at that time was much more suited to be the headquarters- de facto if not de jure - of such a huge firm. It was from London that the eleven overseas branches were administered, though technically they came directly under the Secretary; all the general books, the children's books (which won many prizes), medical, music, and very importantly the ever expanding series of books and dictionaries for teaching English overseas were published.

The London office was first opened for the distribution of the Authorized or King James Bible. OUP is one of the three publishers- with the Cambridge University Press, and the Queen's Printers, now Eyre and Spottiswoode, licensed to publish this version of the Bible (probably the world's bestseller). This privilege was retained when the Revised Version was published, queues of would-be buyers massing outside the London distributing office.

The London office moved in 1922 to a seventeenth-century house, called Amen House. It was built over the ruins of the City walls, themselves forming part of the original Roman wall. I was often asked about its history and the reason for its unusual name, so I asked permission to research into this. I was not quite certain how to begin, so I went to the

Guildhall Library. Their kind librarian gave me excellent advice. 'Look at the deeds,' he said. I then appealed to the Assistant Publisher and inquired where these were to be found. 'Oh, the lawyers should have them,' he answered rather vaguely. I rang them up, but three days later they phoned me back to say that they had searched everywhere, but they were nowhere to be found. As they were of course of immense importance, they were extremely worried. 'Dear me,' said Mr Goffin, 'perhaps they are at the bank in Oxford?'

Sure enough, there they were. As they were irreplaceable, I needed to spend the day at Oxford viewing them at Lloyds Bank. I was terrified that after all this palaver they would be in such obscure language or even in Latin, that I would not be able to decipher them. A huge roll was produced for me in archaic script - late seventeenth century - but in English and I could read it with slight difficulty. The Guildhall librarian was right, from this beginning I was able to piece together the history of the house and the land on which it was built from Roman times. I edited the history of Amen House into a booklet which we gave to interested visitors.

The Romans had built a great wall around the City and a small section was actually found in our cellars. (Indeed a workman once told me that he had seen a helmeted Roman soldier down there when he was painting our canteen!). The house backed on the Old Bailey, formerly Newgate Prison, and these dark rooms on the western side used in my time for the postal workers, were spooky at night. Indeed once when a security guard spent the night there, guarding some treasure for an exhibition, he told me that he had been terrified!

The original house was built by the great Earl of Warwick - the Kingmaker - hence the name Warwick Square. From him it passed to his daughter Anne Neville, the queen of Richard III and thus to the Crown. Like most of the City it was burned to the ground in 1666. It was at this point that the deeds were all important. From the location it described on the Roman wall, I was able to discover the original grant of land after the Fire of London, and it also listed the successive owners. The name Amen House came from the original Amen Corner, one of a succession of such names - Paternoster Square, Ave Maria Lane, Paternoster Row, Creed Lane, Sermon Lane - which evidently marked the pre-Reformation route around old St Paul's for feast day processions. I had a hand in preserving the name Paternoster Square for posterity, after the rebuilding of this part of London after the Blitz. Just before the new square was opened, I strolled around it and saw to my amazement that it had now been called 'Cathedral Square'. I wrote to *The Times* pointing out that there were Cathedral Squares all over the world, but nowhere else was there a Paternoster Square. The letter was not published but a few days later I received a phone call from the Dean of St. Paul's, to whom my letter had been passed, who said he quite agreed with me and would take the matter up with the authorities. The name was changed.

The London office was forced to move in 1965. The Old Bailey had so many cases due I suppose to the increase of crime, that they needed extra courts. After an Act of Parliament, we moved to Ely House, the former eighteenth-century town house of the bishops of Ely. (This had originally been at Ely Place, Holborn. All that remains of it is the chapel, now the Roman Catholic church of St. Etheldreda. It is mentioned in Shakespeare's Richard III for its fine garden of strawberries.)

One of the advantages of being a librarian is that you are always given the loveliest room in the building. The library at Ely House, formerly the drawing room, was superb with three tall mullioned windows looking over Dover Street and slant-wise towards Brown's Hotel. Mrs Chapman the then Secretary's wife, had cleverly picked up exquisite antiques such as a grandfather clock, as well as a seventeenth-century Delft inkstand at knock down prices, when OUP moved to Amen House in 1922. These showed to special advantage in Ely House, when the library was frequently used for launch parties for new books, and other entertainments. I met many interesting authors and personalities at these parties and when they were waiting for appointments.

When I joined the OUP we also distributed from London titles from a large number of the most scholarly and famous university presses in the USA - Harvard, Princeton, Johns Hopkins, Columbia - to mention just a few, as well as those issued by our branches, the largest and most prestigious being OUP New York. Thus the OUP catalogue which I edited for about 25 years, listed some 17,000 books. As librarian I also had to be conversant with the out of print titles, which dated back 500 years! Visitors came to the library to see what was available and to browse to their heart's content. As well as interesting people the occasional madman visited me. I remember one such, who cornered my young assistant and me in a bay of the library, and began to talk about murders he would commit! Another time a young man walked in with a sack over his shoulder like a sailor. He off-loaded this and piles of papers fell all over the floor. 'these are my poems' he said. I saw at a glance they consisted of cut-up sections of hymns, or other men's poems, stuck together haphazardly. 'I want you to publish my works' he said, 'they are wonderful.' 'You'd better select the best ones' I temporized, 'and submit them with a covering letter.' 'Not at all' he replied, 'they might be stolen. Meanwhile, I want you to house them, they are so valuable!' By this time I had edged near the telephone and rung the Religious Editor Geoffrey Hunt, who managed to get rid of him somehow.

Though my main work was as librarian, I gradually got drawn into many different sections of the Press - proof-reading, publicity work, reading submitted manuscripts, if they were on subjects that I was conversant with and many general inquiries, mostly over the telephone. Once I was asked to advise on a nice modern college at Oxford for a foreigner to send his son. He suggested New College and would not believe me, when I told him it was one of the oldest. Another time a Japanese wrote and asked me for a picture of the cave where Bruce met the spider? Strangely enough this was surprisingly easy. Evidently the supposed refuge was not in Scotland but in Northern Ireland and as the Ulster Office was next door to Ely House, we actually found a photo and sent it out to him.

Probably the most interesting work that I became involved with was the new translation of the Bible, called *The New English Bible* (or NEB for short). This was an entirely new translation. About once a month a group of scholars would meet in the Conference Room, which was next door to my library at Amen House. They were the literary panel who would read through the newly translated Bible, chapter by chapter, to make sure that it sounded well in modern but not unacceptably modern language. The team consisted of Dr. C.H. Dodd the General Director, Sir Godfrey Driver Regius Professor of Hebrew at Oxford (and the son of a Regius Professor before him), the then Bishop of Winchester

(Alwyn Williams), Dr. Milner White the Dean of York, and others. At lunchtime they would come and browse in the library and chat with me, discussing the problems in the translation that they had had to overcome.

Sir Godfrey told me that it was the Old Testament that particularly needed retranslating, as at the time when the Authorized Version came out (in 1611), many contemporary sources of manuscripts mostly in the Middle East had not been found. 'Sections of the Old Testament' he said, 'bits you've probably never read, are nonsense. The seventeenth-century scholars had not access to the papers which are now available to us, coming from remote sources such as the Dead Sea Scrolls and from St. Katherine's Monastery.' Dr. Milner White as well as being a Bible expert, was a great musicologist and had been responsible earlier in his life, when he had been Precentor at King's College, Cambridge for starting the service of Nine Carols and Lessons, which are now used universally, and ecumenically at Christmas time. He spent one lunch hour reading through the Magnificat in the library to make certain it would be in the right rhythm for singing.

There were special services in Westminster Abbey to mark the publication in 1961 of the New Testament and then, in 1970 of the completed Bible. On the second occasion, I helped Elizabeth Knight the Publicity Manager, to seat the hundreds of eminent churchmen of all denominations, and other important guests, including the Queen Mother who wanted to attend. It was quite a tricky task as one had to take into account physical disabilities - such as deafness. Then one of the translators, Professor McHardy was in a wheelchair. He had to climb into the high pulpit to read a lesson, not too easy as the marble floor was so highly polished. Sir Godfrey too was a problem as he had a 'dicky' heart and a doctor needed to be on hand in case of an emergency. In fact, everything went smoothly and the New English Bible had phenomenal sales. I even remember seeing men reading copies in the tube!

One amusing interview took place at this time in the library. Professor McHardy was to be questioned by a Canadian radio company about the translation. The Professor was on one side of my desk in his wheelchair, while his interviewer sat opposite him. I was in front of them in my usual chair with the cameramen. I had tried to think of everything which might interrupt the programme, so that there would be complete silence stopping phone calls, visitors etc., but I had quite forgotten the grandfather clock. The interview began well, then noon arrived and the clock began its sonorous twelve chimes. 'Cut!' shouted the Director. 'Why?' objected the effects man, ' I thought it sounded mighty British!'

A light side of OUP life was the Dramatic Society. Unlike most such societies it had no rules and often anyone who could act, sing, or mimic, would be drawn in to take part. Usually there were a series of short plays, or a pantomime at Christmas and there was always one major play, which took place in a professional theatre in the Barbican, in the summer. We put on a splendid masque in honour of the retirement of Mr. Cumberlege. It was called *Scholarship Triumphant or Ye Press Portrayed*, Being a True and Faithfull Dramatick Presentation of ye Genesis, Growth, and Finall Triumph of ye Oxford Universitie Press. John Bell wrote the music and script. As it was 1956 soon after the conquest of Everest, the story was featured around a search for the Abominable Snowmen, who turned out all to be members of the Cambridge University Press in disguise trying to foil an OUP team climbing Mount Everest! A stage was erected in the library and work seems to have been totally forgotten for quite a few days. I suppose it was not very businesslike, but it made for a wonderful atmosphere in the London office.

One day a manuscript arrived in a roughly tied brown paper parcel. When opened it was found to have been entirely written by hand and all in capitals. Luckily John Bell, the General Books Editor, read further and discovered it was the hitherto unknown letters of Wilfred Owen the First World War poet, to his mother. His brother Harold had discovered them in the attic of their home when their mother died. They were of immense interest to scholars, as Wilfred had written almost every day, to his mother from about 1910 to his tragic death just before Armistice Day 1918. John Bell asked me to

Ely House, Dover Street, London

check and write most of the very many footnotes. It was fascinating work as I had to research for instance, many of the references to battlefields in France from the contemporary newspapers. Once I even had to ring the zoo to find out how many teeth a particular tiger he mentioned possessed!

The departments that had been in London were all moved to Oxford by the early eighties.

16

Some Travel Stories

In these early post-war years we began to travel abroad again. During the early 50's one was allowed to export very little currency and in any event none of us had much money. One particular lean year the allowance was only £25 - little even at this period. We sadly thought a foreign holiday would be impossible, but then a letter arrived from a kind Spanish friend we had met through an English professor's introduction the year before. She offered to lend us her largish house in Pollensa, Majorca, for £10 for a month which included the services of her delightful cook Catalina. Off we went and had a delightful time. Our Spanish was basic in the extreme but we managed to chat to Catalina, who told us about her experiences, when she fled from Lluch with her children chased by the Reds. One day my linguistic skill did let me down. We wanted some more butter, so I went into a little shop and asked for some *burro*? I thought the shopkeeper looked rather surprised, so I tried to explain that it was to put on bread. The whole shop of normally rather solemn Spaniards, began to laugh uproariously and I realized that I had used the Italian word and that *burro* in Spanish means donkey. I should have said *mantequilla*!

Every day we took a bus to Pollensa Bay and then a ferry to Formentor, even then the site of an expensive hotel far beyond our pockets. However, Catalina cooked us delicious Spanish omelettes, which we ate on the lovely beach under the shade of Mediterranean palms. Our Spanish friends who were at their country villa at Cala d'Or, arrived one day and drove us over there. We met her mother and father. He had been Spanish ambassador in Washington right through their Civil War. Living up to my one-time nickname - Candid Anne - I actually asked him how he had managed to survive both under the Republic and then under General Franco? He was unabashed and said that everything had gone on much as usual - a Spanish Vicar of Bray.

Next year we nearly ran out of money on a visit to Italy. The last day we spent in Rome, having our return tickets to England and for the open-air opera in the Baths of Caracalla. However, by lunchtime we began to feel hungry and spied a small pavement restaurant near the Spanish Steps. We had no money. Then Sheila searched among the jewellery she had with her and produced a small piece of jade. She boldly went into very grand jeweller's shop and asked I think the owner whether he would like to buy it? 'I will give you - lire,' he agreed. Not much but it was just enough to pay for a meal at the trattoria we had seen. We saw him looking very amused, when he spotted us ensconced there a few minutes later as he drove by in a superb limousine to a no doubt very grand lunch!

A great change to our life and subsequent holidays came in 1957, when ICI unexpectedly gave me £300 for my shares with them - the equivalent of about £3,000 of today's money. My friend, Eleanor Macnair had just bought a Messerschmidt a little three-wheeled bullet-like German car and I decided to buy the other model, called a Heinkel. They were nicknamed 'bubble cars'. My Heinkel was shaped like a fat pear seating three thin people in front. The gears including a reverse were on a sort of stick. The roof lifted up from the side to allow one to enter or leave. All our friends warned us that it was very dangerous, as it had virtually no protection, not much acceleration, and was extremely low on the ground. Moreover my Ceylonese driving licence had not only been lost on the journey home, but was, in any case out of date.

Undeterred, I bought my Heinkel but was of course unable to drive it alone until I had passed the British driving test. First I needed experience. I had not driven for fifteen years and traffic in Ceylon was not to be compared with that in central London during a bus strike, which happened to be raging at that moment. Also I found that no ordinary driving school would agree to teach a learner driver in a bubble car. Luckily a colleague's father owned a garage and one of his driving instructors bravely agreed to teach me. The next hurdle was to gain experience. I discovered a man in the postal department of the OUP with a licence, who lived near Dolphin Square. In return for a free ride, he was happy to drive with me every day to work. This practice was invaluable but one day the telephonist took me aside and whispered that I should beware of driving with X as he had a bad reputation! What this reputation was I never discovered but as my licensed passenger was an ex-schoolmaster in a lowly job, I could only assume there might have been homosexual troubles (at that time illegal). In any case I instantly decided that my virtue was unlikely to be in danger in a bubble car driving between Dolphin Square, Westminster, and St Paul's and driving experience was well worth any risk! Actually he was an extremely nice man and a very good teacher. I am sure I owe as much to his quiet instruction, as I do to the four lessons by the official driving instructor.

The all-important day of the test arrived in 1957. I drove with my instructor to Merton, where we went over the likely test area. I was so nervous of failing that I made every mistake possible on this trial drive and my teacher thought I would certainly fail. I arrived at the office and was greeted by a genial and very large ex-police officer who was to examine me. He had never travelled in a bubble before and could hardly squeeze in beside me on the right side. Being a German car it had a left hand drive.

I proceeded cautiously down the Merton road, when the indicator turned red to show I needed to switch for more petrol - a peculiarity of the Heinkels. I explained this and pulled in to move the lever. The examiner turned to me and said, 'How is it that you are an experienced driver and yet I see this is your first test?' I explained that I had driven before in Sri Lanka, but my licence had lapsed in the war and we drove on. All my confidence was restored by this question and I made no mistakes. When we arrived back at the office, my ex-policeman showed me his black book which was blank. 'Provided you answer the statutory questions you have passed' he said. These were no problem and it was one of the happiest days of my life. I had the liberty of the road!

We soon began to holiday abroad by car. The first venture was for the three of us my mother, Sheila and me to set off in the bubble to the Netherlands for the Easter weekend of 1958. We sat side by side in the front seat with our luggage stacked behind and sailed for the Hook of Holland. Actually the Low Countries were a good choice as all the lovely cities - Amsterdam, The Hague, Haarlem - are so close together. At that time parking mostly, somewhat dangerously by the canals was unrestricted and traffic was minimal. It was tremendous fun though I was a bit nervous. We also had the opportunity of visiting Elizabeth, née

Ogilvie (who I had known in Delhi in 1942) now married to a charming Dutchman, Frans Laaman Trip, who she met when they were both in Edinburgh University at the end of the war. They lived in the country and we drove there in our tiny car on minor roads beside the many canals that criss-cross the land. I had never realized before the reason that the Dutch painters were able to achieve such marvellous sky effects with these flat landscapes and huge amounts of visible sky. These we could see so well from bubble level.

On Easter Sunday we decided to cross the Nordsee Canal by ferry. I had forgotten that the Heinkel was a German car and was surprised when the ticket collector gave me a very black look. We were used to the friendliness displayed to the English. He walked around the minute car with a scowl, until suddenly he saw the GB plate, when his face completely changed. He rushed back to me and shook us all warmly by the hand refusing to charge for our passage. The Germans at this time, were extremely unpopular in Holland. The Dutch had before the war, considered them as friends, and had taken in German children after World War I to help them, and many Hollanders had been educated in Germany. The invasion and occupation, so vividly portrayed in *The Diary of Anne Frank*, had now made them very hostile to Germans. An English army friend of mine using a German car was deliberately misdirected about this time, due to this attitude.

I traded the bubble for a Fiat Cinquecento after nine months and for the first time owned a 'proper' car. My friends were relieved but actually I have never again either bought a Fiat or a second-hand car, as everything that could go wrong went wrong while the Heinkel had worked perfectly. The worst time was when we attempted to cross the Pyrenees into Andorra, when it just stopped. Eventually we did reach the pass, but I soon cut my losses and bought one of the first Minis, thereafter progressing to slightly larger cars as my finances improved.

17

Sheila enters the Foreign Service

Soon after the war, in 1948, the Attlee government set up a department called the Information Research Department (IRD) under the Foreign Office. Its object was to combat Russian Communist propaganda, which with the onset of the Cold War, was engaged in a damaging global campaign against the Western World. It is perhaps difficult to realize now that British public opinion was still extremely pro-Russia. After all 'Uncle Joe' had been our ally for many years and indeed his victories had contributed enormously to the Allied victory. Moreover, the Attlee government was Socialist and many of their MPs were sympathetic towards communism. The Foreign Office, however, saw the dangers. Christopher Warner Assistant Under Secretary of State at that time wrote a paper in 1946 called, 'The Soviet campaign against this country and our response to it'.

Attlee was favourably disposed to the idea but Bevin the Foreign Secretary, thought the proposals were too negative - 'The more I study it the less I like it' he wrote. But in 1947 the Soviet propaganda barrage and the attacks in their press on the Labour Party, accusing them of 'stimulating an anti-Soviet propaganda campaign and urging Social democrats to ally with the forces of imperialism' (*Pravda*, 10 June) began to change this attitude. In 1948 Mr. Bevin presented to the Cabinet a memorandum on 'Future Foreign Publicity Policy' together with two interconnected papers. He described the threat to the 'fabric of Western Civilisation' posed by Russia and her Communist allies, and argued that it was for the British Government as European Social democrats and not for the Americans, to give the lead in the spiritual, moral and political sphere to all the democratic elements in Western Europe which were anti-communist and at the same time, genuinely progressive and reformist.

The stage was now set for the establishment of IRD. Specialist staff needed to be recruited, not directly under the Civil Service, and to be paid under the secret vote to avoid undue scrutiny of operations. France and Italy with large communist electorates, were given the first priority for counter-propaganda. All overseas Posts had been asked their opinions as to this new influx of counter propaganda and most had welcomed it. Instead of using pamphlets, as had been used in the war, it was deemed essential that these writings should not be seen as government inspired and that the work of this department should not be known to the British public. Articles were placed in the widest range of weekly newspapers. IRD also helped to secure the publication of a book by a Soviet defector. It also attempted to counter Soviet behaviour in the United Nations and at other international gatherings, where the Russians made long and carefully prepared speeches clearly aimed at a wider audience and having little to do with the current debate. IRD soon had important links with the BBC and the COI (The Central Office of Information).

Sheila had now spent ten years at Chatham House and Peter Calvocoressi realized that she was not ideal for the work in which they were engaged, as speed was essential for the strict timetable needed to produce the *Annual Surveys*. Sheila, at this time was not a quick writer, as she was too prone to check and research her work. He therefore decided it was time for her to leave Chatham House.

However, as so often I have found in life, everything proved for the best. Peter had influential friends in the Foreign Office including I believe Christopher Warner, and Sheila was taken on immediately in IRD. Apart from her academic qualifications, as she had worked throughout the war with secret documents, her security status was unimpeachable. Soon she rose to head her department initially on the Far East. She worked very hard and her experience both at writing and in foreign affairs was soon recognized.

In 1958 she was sent on a visit to South-East Asia to gain knowledge of these countries-Burma, Thailand, Vietnam, etc. She met many influential people, as well as visiting the vast ancient ruins of Ankhor Wat. On her way home she managed to have a break in Beirut over Easter and visit

Jerusalem, still under Jordanian rule. She had expected to stay there with the British Consul, but the message had never arrived. Thus, when Sheila arrived on Good Friday morning she found the consulate closed and every hotel room filled, as it happened to be the Orthodox as well as the Western Easter. By chance, our vicar, Tony Tremlett, (later Bishop of Dover), had given her an introduction to the Anglican Archbishop in Jerusalem and Metropolitan, Angus Campbell Macinnes. She rang him up and asked if it would be possible to leave her cases in his palace while she searched for accommodation. 'Come and stay with us', he said, 'a visitor has just cancelled, so we have a spare bed.' Sheila was thrilled and enjoyed a fascinating weekend. The archbishop and his wife were the kindest of hosts and the archbishop took Sheila to two most unusual services in the Church of the Holy Sepulchre.

The first was a mass sung by the Ethiopian pontiff, whose section of the great building is sited on its roof. The bishop and priests actually danced before the altar of the Lord - as King David had done in Old Testament times - while minute black acolytes, dressed only in tiny purple velvet cloaks, followed them waving incense. The second service was the Greek Orthodox Midnight Mass. Here all the worshippers lit candles from each other, shouting 'Christ is risen, He is risen indeed!' with such excitement that Sheila was afraid that her hair would be set alight! During the days she was in Jerusalem a biblical scholar, who was also a house guest, took her around many of the most famous Christian sites.

18

Sheila in the Diplomatic Service

It was soon after this, in 1961, that Sheila's life was changed by a new decision of the Foreign Office. It was decided that it would be useful to have an information officer at the United Kingdom Mission to the United Nations in New York. Sheila was offered the posting for three years. In the event she stayed for twenty and soon was transferred to the main Diplomatic Service. Before she retired she rose to become a Counsellor, a step below Ministers and Ambassadors and in 1979 President of the 46th Trusteeship Council.

Sheila arrived in New York in 1961 without any experience of diplomatic life. All diplomats have to work long hours, starting with 'Morning prayers' when the days business is discussed, followed by meetings at the UN often lasting late into the night, especially when the Security Council had been convened. But Sheila also had to run her flat, arrange many official dinners and drinks parties as well as to cook for herself at other times. (Diplomats' wives normally handle these latter activities.) Sheila had had good experience in entertaining, when we lived at Trinco, as we did a great deal of entertaining there, and she soon became well known in New York for her ability to mix members from widely different countries and ethnic groups with a sprinkling of her own friends - often Americans - at her parties. Sheila had a gift of getting on with people throughout her life. She was very pretty with a lovely smile and possessed great charm, but she also had a flair for clothes. I believe she was considered one of the best-dressed women in the UN. One of her fellow female diplomats who served with her in New York, laughingly told me that however suddenly they were called to the Security Council or an emergency meeting in the early morning, while most of them would arrive looking fairly untidy, Sheila would always appear as if she had come straight from Elizabeth Arden's salon!

Kindness was one of the other of Sheila's characteristics, which endeared her to everyone. Many ex-ambassadors etc. have told me how she was always ready to help Third World officials, newly arrived at the UN on matters such as procedure, protocol, or even what to wear at social functions. She was so gentle that they were never afraid to approach her for advice, knowing that they could trust her to give them a helpful and truthful answer, without thinking she was trying to influence the way they would vote in the Assembly. Probably her actions would be of inestimable value to Great Britain.

This kindness extended beyond her official position. For instance she once invited her maid to bring her two children to lunch in the Delegates' Dining room at the United Nations - a treat they would probably never forget. On other occasions she visited employees in Harlem Hospital (in the Black quarter of New York City,) when they were ill. She also read for the blind.

Her role when she had first been sent to New York had been as an adviser on Cold War questions, which she had acquired during her apprenticeship at Chatham House and in IRD. Indeed her memory was formidable, but it was quite soon realized by successive ambassadors that should a tricky problem arise, or someone difficult needed to be dealt with, it would be suggested ' Let's send Sheila to deal with him (or her)!' Mr. Kharlamov, (Union of Soviet Socialist Republics) said of her, when she later ended her year as President of the Trusteeship Council 'I should like to thank Miss Harden the previous President, for the charm and tact with which she has conducted the affairs of the Trusteeship Council. If a woman were always President of the Trusteeship Council I do not think the male portion of the population would feel offended thereby, for the presence of a woman as President of our Council would have a restraining effect on us in our emotional reactions, our evaluations and our criticisms of whatever shortcomings we might encounter in examining the issues connected with Trusteeship.'

One of Sheila's most important and difficult assignments was when she made contact with one of the newly arrived Chinese officials. The People's Republic of China had superseded Taiwan's Nationalist Republic of China in the UN in 1971. They were on very bad terms with the USA, who had supported Chiang Kai Shek, and so relations between these two great powers were strained in the extreme. Great Britain had recognized the People's Republic before the Korean War. Thus Sheila's diplomacy with the new Chinese communist government was particularly valuable and used by successive British ambassadors. She came to be on excellent terms with Chou Nan an important member of the new Chinese delegation.

Sheila should have left New York after the normal diplomatic term of three years, but as each ambassador replaced another, they each refused to part with Sheila. They needed her memory and experience, as she was the one member of their staff with continuity of service. For instance, a situation might arise on Central Asia which had arisen ten or so years before, but nobody could remember quite how it had been dealt with. Formerly the Mission would have had to phone or telegraph London - no e-mails or faxes then - to request the relevant details of the previous crisis. Instead someone would suggest that Sheila might be asked. Sure enough she would usually be able to find the relevant documents and explain what had been the policy on the former occasion. This sort of knowledge would save days of inquiry and usually the information was needed at once.

Sheila behind Sir Patrick Dean, the British ambassador, at the United Nations

To quote from John Sankey: 'I arrived in New York just after Sheila, and remember in particular her contribution to a speech by Sir Patrick Dean in the General Assembly debate on decolonisation in 1962. The Soviet delegate had been more than usually offensive so Sheila produced some pertinent references to Soviet Central Asia.

Pat Dean pointed out that Kazakhstan and Turkmenistan had been annexed in the middle of the 19th century, just at the time when Britain was taking control of the Gold Coast and Nigeria. These two former British colonies were now independent; when would Kazakhstan and Turkmenistan be independent?

The Soviet delegate was furious, and Sheila had scored a bull's-eye. (Little did she and I then dream that we would see Kazakhstan and Turkmenistan become independent members of the U.N. thirty years later in 1992.)

Another of her 'discoveries' were the Kurile Islands off the coast of Japan, which Russia had illegally occupied in 1945 and no one had heard of until she 'outed' them. Hugh Foot recalls in his memoirs how he used the Kuriles to tease the Soviets. Their return to the then Soviet Union was one of Stalin's conditions for belatedly entering the Second World War on the Allied side. (The unfortunate islanders were either slaughtered or sent to death camps in Siberia.)

Although Sheila enjoyed making the Soviet delegates uncomfortable, she came to their rescue on one occasion. During an interminable Soviet speech on colonialism, the UN interpreter loosely translated a Russian proverb, as 'something is rotten in the State of Denmark'. The Danish delegate who had been listening with only one ear, heard his country mentioned and angrily interrupted on a point of order to ask why the Soviet Union was accusing his country of colonialism? The Soviet delegate was completely baffled, but Sheila as usual had been fully alert and was able to explain it was a quotation from Hamlet and avert a minor row.'

Sheila's first ambassador was Sir Patrick Dean. He and his wife Patricia were extremely kind to her and their helpfulness must have been a tower of strength to her then, when everything including being in a new country, must have seemed very strange. Diplomats were allowed to choose their own accommodation which was paid by the Foreign Office, according to rank. Thus Sheila's flats - she changed apartments five times - became increasingly large to allow her room for entertaining foreign diplomats to drink parties and dinners. For these she was able to employ an excellent Spanish cook and her husband, who acted as butler.

I think the general public tend to regard all these official parties as one around of gaiety and drinking. In fact, they are a very important means for diplomats to sound the views of other delegations and the voting intentions in the General Assembly in more relaxed and discreet surroundings than in the corridors of the UN building. Indeed very few of them drank much and a great many nationals particularly Asians and Moslems, never touched alcohol. Often there would be as many as three parties in one evening, so perhaps it was just as well.

Much of Sheila's time was spent in her office, writing reports, researching information for ambassadorial speeches and at morning meetings, and discussing the line the varying British governments wished pursued on the issues of the moment. Later in the day or occasionally, quite early if the Security Council had been convened, Sheila would go down to the UN building, a few blocks from the UK Mission and sit behind the ambassador or his deputy at Security Council or General Assembly meetings. Though the General Assembly speeches could be dull and repetitious, Sheila always had to be prepared for the unexpected.

For instance once quite early in her time in New York, all the more senior members of the British Mission were absent at lunch and Sheila was temporarily representing the UK. Unexpectedly, the Argentinean ambassador rose in his place and claimed the Falklands for his country. Sheila was not caught off her guard replying that the 'United Kingdom has no intention of yielding sovereignty of these islands to the Republic of the Argentine.' This incident happened years before the Falklands War and was I imagine not an unusual maneuver by the Argentine government, but it was a 'first' for Sheila!

In 1965 the Mission was asked for an observer to be sent by the UK government to an Asian conference to be held in Outer Mongolia, at Ulan Bator, on the Rights of Women in Public Life. Sheila suggested to her ambassador Lord Caradon, that as she was the only woman accredited to the Mission at that moment, she would be a good member to send. A trip to Outer Mongolia would be the chance of a lifetime. Lord Caradon readily agreed and Sheila made her travel arrangements. She cleverly discovered that it would actually be cheaper for the taxpayer if she took an around the world excursion, for Ulan Bator was about equidistant from New York. She stopped first with us in London and then in an RAF plane, flew via Denmark to Moscow. She stayed with a diplomat there and he arranged for her to visit St. Petersburg - then Leningrad - with a somewhat staid if learned historian, who was arranging an exhibition from the Hermitage. At that time the Cold War was very real. Sheila said that when she asked for directions people just turned their backs on her. When she reached the rendezvous at the Moscow Station she discovered that she and the professor had been given a double-berth compartment. He was so modest that he was prepared to sit up all night. Sheila was not so prudish and suggested that he could go into the corridor, while she undressed, and thereafter they would both have a good night's sleep!

Back to Moscow without the professor, she flew on to Lake Baykal in Siberia, where she joined the Trans-Siberian railway, as one branch turns south there towards Peking via Ulan Bator. (Its name means Red Hero.) At this time Mongolia was still very primitive. It had been admitted to the United Nations in 1961. The country is 600,000 square miles in size (three times the size of France) and has a population of 2 million, two-thirds being farmers and cattle minders, who live almost entirely in yurts, cone shaped, lattice structures constructed from felt and canvas. However, since Sheila's visit they were the first Asian country to grant women full equality and women now make up a quarter of deputies in the Great People's Khural, in their Supreme Court, and 70% of medical personnel. The only hotel then was an enormous guesthouse some five miles outside the town. It could accommodate up to three or four hundred people and was used by visiting delegations, including our Minister Reginald Hibbert (the late Sir Reginald.) Sheila stayed there with him and his wife Ann. As it was almost the only building, everything including all the seminars took place here. The Mongolians were very excited at sponsoring such a conference and I gathered from Sheila, did everything in their power to entertain their guests. The only other European observers were from the Eastern bloc. One of these washed Sheila's hair. Sheila was normally very particular and always went to Elizabeth Arden in New York. She told me afterwards that she had never had such a strange coiffure!

They held a wonderful long distance horse race on their beautiful and very fast horses. The jockeys are always quite young children, who are chosen for their lightness and to prove the excellence of the steeds rather than the skill of the horsemen. However, as Mongolians learn to ride practically from birth, Sheila thought that the little riders must take a good deal of credit for their wins. The plain, with small hills is very beautiful in the short summer and covered with masses of wild flowers and grassy slopes, a bit like the Sussex Downs. Ann Hibbert interested herself, during her husband's periods in Ulan Bator, in painting and cataloguing the local flora and fauna. But in the winter the temperature can drop to 40 degrees below zero Fahrenheit. Another time the visitors were taken to a banquet in a huge yurt. Food was laid out on long tables. However, as it mostly consisted of rancid mare's milk *koumiss*, (Sheila anyway could not drink ordinary milk) and equally disgusting food, she had difficulty hiding her helpings so as not to offend her hosts!

When the conference ended Sheila took the Trans-Siberian Railway to Peking (Beijing now). The train was nearly full. Two compartments had been reserved for two Queen's Messengers - senior retired officers who personally carried the diplomatic secret mailbags around the world - and the other first class sleeper was occupied by two French male communists. These Queen's Messengers happened to be on unfriendly terms with each other, but they (metaphorically), pulled their moustaches, and decided grievances between each should be shelved in order to save Sheila from sharing with the Frenchmen. Sheila thought that their horror at this contingency arose neither from fear for her from their sex, nor from the fact that they were communists, but because they were FRENCHMEN! In return for the Queen's Messengers' patriotic unselfishness Sheila made them many cups of tea from the samovars, which were to be found at the end of each corridor. I also think it mended their tiff with each other. Strangely enough a friend of ours Eleanor Macnair, who lives in the New Forest met one of them at a party and they found by chance, that he had travelled with Sheila across Mongolia and China a few days before. A small world indeed!

At Peking, again staying with diplomats Sheila was lucky enough to see the sights including the Great Wall (which she had just passed through) and the Summer Palace without the hordes of tourists, who now invade these places. I am ashamed to say that great-uncle, Pakenham Angelo, (later General) was one of the European contingent who after the Boxer Rising in 1904, took part in the sacking of the Summer Palace and brought back some fabulous treasures from its vast interior! Sheila did not sack Peking but she did find some lovely pictures which she bought. They now hang in my drawing room. As they were not antiques they were allowed through the strict Chinese customs.

She left China via Canton where the atmosphere became very tense, as it was just before the Cultural Revolution. A 'guide' who attempted to show her the new communist built Sports Stadium, while she asked to see ancient monasteries, closely supervised her. In the end there was a compromise and she saw everything. I think the Chinese fears that Sheila might be spying on their military equipment was groundless, as I am sure she would not have known the difference between one aircraft or weapon from another! She completed her around the world trip by visiting Japan and Hawaii.

There was an amusing occurrence in which Sheila took a leading part and which appeared in several New York papers, including *The New York Times* of 29 April 1964. During the World's Fair a replica of the HMS *Bounty* docked in Flushing Bay with a direct descendant of the leader of the mutineers, Fletcher Christian, on board from Pitcairn Island. The UK Mission was asked to send a representative to meet Mr Christian. Sheila happened to be talking to Sir Patrick when this request came through. She laughed and said, ' I ought to go, because I believe that I am descended from Captain Bligh, the captain of the *Bounty*.' Sure enough, she went off to the ceremony and the press were greatly intrigued by this meeting: 'In a gesture of goodwill, these descendants of arch enemies - shook hands to officially open the exhibit.... Later Christian said, " My great-great-great grandfather was a brave man who cherished freedom. What he did was not mutiny. He wanted freedom and justice. That's all." Sheila in reply said "Captain Bligh is painted in books and films as an arrogant even sadistic and sinister villain, but she believes history should be more kind to her ancestor. He was a strict disciplinarian. He upheld the laws of the sea and the code of conduct which existed in his day and pointed to his extraordinary navigational feat in making the 3,000 mile sea voyage in an open boat from the *Bounty* to safety."

Sheila meeting the descendant of Christian Fletcher on board a replica of HMS Bounty in New York Harbour for the World Fair

Sheila very naturally was interested in the position of women at the United Nations, but in 1971 she told *The New York Times* that their numbers were increasing and that now there were some 30 to 40 nations which included women in their delegations, though the diplomatic community remains a male-dominated world. To quote from their issue of 24 August: 'Miss Harden is one of the few who get to handle political items. Her job is the analysis and research that go into preparing for political debate, rather than the speech making, although she does that too.

"Sheila is our memory," said a British representative. He also said she draws some of the touchier assignments, not because anyone believes it would make a change of vote or make an unpopular position more palatable but because "Sheila makes it sound better."

Like most women delegates, Miss Harden objects to the tradition of delegating some topics to women and others to men. "Why shouldn't a woman be interested in disarmament (male topic) or a man in human rights (female topic)?" She asked "The United Nations is an ideal post for a woman. We're rather like a club...we work together... we eat together."

Under the heading The Only Woman *The New York Times* continues 'Frequently at these working luncheons the slim, silver blond British representative is the only woman along with 16 or 17 male companions. "I rather enjoy it," she said "and why not?"

Sitting in her book-cluttered office at the mission, Miss Harden reflected on the changing role of women. She noted that many of the women from the newer countries of Asia and Africa have moved quickly up the career ladder because a young government tends to utilize whatever competent officials are available without worrying about male-female distinctions. But as the pool of experienced officials gets better, she conceded women may find the going tougher.'

In 1967 Sheila received the MBE from Sir Patrick Dean, on behalf of the Queen in Washington. He had by then become British Ambassador to the United States, probably the top diplomatic job. My mother and I were invited to the ceremony at the embassy and afterwards in its beautiful and very English gardens, which were lovingly tended by Sir Patrick.

19

Travels in the Americas

Sheila's departure for America left a great gap in my mother's and my life for unlike most British and American families, ours had always been extremely close. However, as my mother had married at twenty and she was exceedingly young in spirit and enterprising, she came to be in many ways more like a second sister to me. I of course was working at the OUP, but my mother filled her week by becoming a Governor of our parish school - the Burdett Coutts-running a club for old age pensioners, and working for the King George's Fund for Sailors. Then in weekends we would drive to the country to visit friends and relations, or walk in the hills of the Home Counties, and go abroad for short visits including the Holy Land.

However, the really exciting travels for us were the opening of the New World to our eyes. We wasted no time. Sheila arrived in New York early in 1961 and mother and I flew across the Atlantic for the first time that summer. Then there were no jet aircraft and the crossing took about eleven hours. I do not mind admitting that for my first few trans-Atlantic flights I was very scared and mother was even more so, but was it worth it? My goodness!

The first thing that struck me in America was the size of everything - the length of the streets in the cities, the ease of parking (except in New York City) the largeness of the cars and of course the great height of the buildings. Also the vastness of the country so that inhabitants of the west of the USA neither knew, or cared, much about what was happening in the east. But what was universal was the tremendous hospitality and warmth of everybody. Sheila met us at the airport - not yet named The John F. Kennedy, for he was not assassinated until 1963 - and we were whisked through the VIP exit. At that time British visitors had to obtain visitors' visas from the US embassy in Grosvenor Square London, before being allowed entry. One had to sit in a large waiting room and then an official, who sat at a desk in the middle of the room, interrogated us publicly. The first thing he asked in a loud voice was 'What is your weight?' As mother and I were light we did not mind, but a large lady just behind went pink to her eyebrows as she was asked this in stentorian tones! A police friend told me later, that this question is never asked in Europe but actually is a useful identification, as it is hard for a small thin person to assume extra weight and height.

But to return to our arrival in New York. For a few days Sheila showed us the great city and we met some of her friends and colleagues and she also took us to lunch in the Delegates' Lounge of the United Nations. Then she told us that some kind Americans had offered to lend us their country cottage in Maine, just south of the Canadian border. We decided to hire a car for me to drive. America is a car economy and apart from New York it is very difficult to manage without one. As up to now I had only driven my bubble followed by the earliest very tiny minis, and in Trinco a small Ford, driving the vast (to me) automatic Chevrolet was a new and slightly alarming experience. After one trial run on the Saturday with a friend of Sheila's, I set off on Saturday morning alone to pick up the car, only to discover it was an entirely different model from the one I had practised on. 'It's much easier, maam,' said the garage man and left me. John Cambridge a colleague of Sheila's, had invited us to spend the first few nights in his shared country cottage up the Hudson River. The idea was that he with my mother should lead me in his car, while I drove with Sheila as my passenger, out of New York on the parkway north. I followed him gingerly getting the feel of a so much larger car, but laughingly said to Sheila, 'The car hire man never told me how to stop!' Of course I really knew how but Sheila, who was entirely ignorant of cars and the most impractical person in the world, said, 'Will we have to go on then until the petrol runs out?'

Once we reached Sorrento on the Maine coast, we found it was a small peninsula containing perhaps twenty-four summer houses around a small church. Descendants of three men, who had built them in the early twentieth century, owned them all. Our hosts had not only lent us their house but had also phoned many of their neighbours, asking them to befriend us. We made more friends when we attended the church on Sunday. The so-called country cottage was a millionaire's idea of one. Built in wood with a pretty terrace - protected against mosquitoes of which there were many - it contained every modern comfort and was beautifully though simply furnished. We visited many neighbours, including an evening hymn singing party at the Canadian ambassador, Tommy Stone's house. I am afraid that Sheila and I were very bad representatives of Great Britain as we were and are almost tone deaf; and though mother had a lovely though largely untrained voice, many of the hymns were unfamiliar. However, nobody seemed to mind.

Two years later, when we were coming out to the States again Sheila happened to meet Tommy Stone at a charity garden party for English gentlewomen stranded in the USA, which she had nearly skipped, but had decided to attend out of duty. She was well rewarded. Tommy inquired whether we were coming out to America and when Sheila said that we had thought of visiting the Deep South, he immediately offered to lend us his ranch near Charleston in South Carolina. He was only sorry that he would not be there. It was wonderfully kind. We drove south via Williamsburg and Washington and arrived at his plantation about a week later. It was *Gone with the Wind* country. Not only had Tommy told his factor to buy all the food for us, but his two servants both descended from former family slaves looked after us. There was an elderly cook and a young man, who took over driving the car then changed his hat to wait at table. They both adored the Stone family and could not do enough for us. Tommy had also telephoned his friends and they asked us over. In the church the old Confederate flag of the South, hung beside the Stars and Stripes by the altar. It was interesting to see how the old best relationship which had existed between the kindest masters and their slaves, survived though in such a different form. The loyalty remained but with no subservience and the young man turned up in a car about twice the size of mine at home! The other thing that was interesting was told me by one of the friends we met. They could trace the part of Africa from which the early slaves had come by the handicrafts they still made, which came from parts of their original homelands.

In later years we explored the west of the United States, the Rockies and the canyons, as well as much of Canada, Peru, and Mexico. In the sixties and the seventies, there were very few British travellers in these parts in the countryside. (There were, of course, many businessmen who went to the cities.) I remember at one talk in a huge stadium in the open air in

California, at the end the lecturer asked if there were any folk from the eastern United States? A dozen or so put up their hands. Then he said 'Is there anyone here from Europe?' and only I think five raised their hands. Then he asked where we came from? When we said Britain, the whole amphitheatre cheered and the couple behind us said, 'We were mighty proud to be sitting behind you.' It was very warming.

We had a few adventures on these forays over the Americas. In Mexico we went down a long series of subterranean caves, only to have the lights extinguished when we were half a mile down them. I think the guides hoped to make us all give money to restart the electricity. However, their plans were foiled as a Frenchman had a cigarette lighter. In Peru we went up the Amazon in a tiny boat, just large enough for the boatman and us. Suddenly the engine stopped and we began turning around and around. As the river was full of piranhas and crocodiles, we were not keen on sinking. The boatman indicated that I should take the wheel, while he tried to get the engine going. As I could not remember whether you had to steer like a sailing boat, or like a car, we continued to drift. However, all was well and we reached the very primitive hotel set in the heart of the jungle. At this time mother was eighty and gamely trekked through the undergrowth watching the wildlife with us.

However, our doctor much to her annoyance had forbidden her to go up to Machu Picchu, which is at an altitude of some 8,000 feet, so Sheila and I arranged for her to go ahead of us to the white city of Arequipa in the south of Peru. I do not think that we had realized that she had never travelled alone before and when she arrived at the airport in Lima for Arequipa, she must have looked rather forlorn. A very kind middle-aged American couple came up to her and asked if she would like to travel with them. They arranged for her to change planes and looked after her for the next two days until Sheila and I arrived. It turned out that they were Mormons and had come to Peru for a two-year sabbatical to help the local people. He was a lawyer. I had always been rather suspicious of Mormons before this but it shows that the words, by your works ye shall know them, is perfectly true.

While Sheila and I were at the extraordinarily magnificent site of Machu Picchu, far away from everyone you would think, Sheila suddenly heard her name called, 'Sheila!' It turned out to be the Belgian ambassador to

Peru, who was also visiting Machu Picchu with his wife. They were charming and showed us all around Lima a few days later.

In the airport in Cuzco we had been held up by engine trouble for some hours and could not reach Arequipa, where we knew mother would be anxiously waiting for us. It was not more than about forty miles away but was separated by an impenetrable range of the Andes. Sheila saw a woman who looked as if she might speak English and so approached her. Indeed she was a Canadian and explained everything to us. We then invited her to have some coffee. In conversation we asked her what her job was? 'I'm a nun' she answered. We must have looked surprised as she was wearing a local poncho and trousers. 'It would be absurd for my sister and me to wear habits and coifs', she said, ' we would spend all day laundering them and besides one couldn't ride mules properly. We are teaching the local women to market their beautiful knitwear, so that the garments can be sold profitably in the States and Canada.'

Perhaps the most dangerous adventure Sheila and I had was in the Rockies - in the Glacier National Park. We were walking down a narrow path high in the mountains, when we came around a bend and Sheila suddenly exclaimed, 'There's a bear!' Sure enough, across the path, about twenty-five yards ahead of us was an enormous grizzly. There were a lot of notices about grizzlies. They are carnivorous and had killed a number of back-packers the previous year, but normally one did not see them in the mountains, only in cars in the lower parts of the parks such as Yellowstone.

The Grizzly bear we met on a path in Glacier National Park.

We backed around the curve and wondered what to do, as we had to get past him to reach our car a mile or so away. At that moment an American couple appeared, the first people we had seen all day. We explained the predicament. The woman said, 'Let's have a peek at him!' We advanced gingerly again around the corner and there was the bear, who now began advancing quite fast towards us. The man picked up a stick and so did Shcila and I took a stone, while the woman who had a camera slung around her neck bravely took a photo. We backed away but the bear gained on us, so we turned down towards the river and he turned too. Suddenly he got bored and vanished! A week or so later the couple sent us the photo, which proved that it had been a grizzly which we had encountered and not a more usual brown bear. Should a grizzly catch you, it is almost certain death.

My mother, Sheila, and me at the Columbia Glacier, Canada, where the rivers flow to the Atlantic, Pacific, and Arctic Oceans.

20

Micronesia

Europeans first discovered Micronesia, consisting of more than 2,100 islands and atolls, scattered over an area of some 3 million square miles of the western Pacific Ocean, north of the Equator in 1521. The islands which have a combined land area of only 707 square miles, form three major archipelagos - the Marianas, the Carolines, and the Marshalls - and are collectively known as Micronesia.

When Magellan with his three tiny ships, the *Trinidad*, the *Victoria*, and the *Conception*, landed at Guam in 1521 a crew member, Antonio Pigafetta wrote an account of this island and its inhabitants: 'On Wednesday the 6th of March we discovered a small island in the northwest direction, and two others lying to the

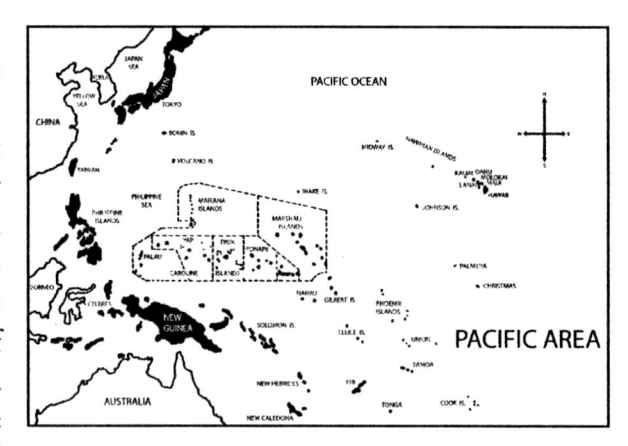

Pacific area map showing the Micronesian Islands.

southwest...these people live in freedom. Some of them wear beards and have hair down to their waist. They wear small hats, like the Albanians; these hats are made of palm leaves. The people are as tall as us and well built. They worship no god. When they are born they are white; later they become brown. Their teeth are black and red. The women go naked except that they cover their loins with a thin bark as soft as paper, which grows beneath the bark of the palm. They wear their hair loose and flowing; it is very black and long. They do not go to work in the fields nor stir from their houses, but make cloth and baskets of palm leaves. Their food consists of coconuts, potatoes, birds, figs, as long as the palm of a hand, sugar cane and flying fish. The women anoint their bodies and their hair with oil made from coconuts and flowers. Their houses are constructed of wood and covered with planks and fig leaves, which are three yards in length. They have only one floor; their rooms and beds are furnished with mats made of palm leaves and are very beautiful. They lie down on palm straw which is soft and fine. These people have no weapons but use sticks that have a fish bone at the end. They are poor but ingenious and also great thieves. For this reason we called these islands the Ladrone Islands (Islands of Thieves).'

Sheila did not consider them to be thieves, (which, of course, they were not!), but became immensely attached to these islands, and many of their people to her over the next years, while she helped to organize their independence referenda.

By 1967 when Sheila first began to deal with the Trusteeship Council, Micronesia was the last Trust Territory. After she had retired from Directorship of the David Davies Institute in 1995, she wrote a Project Proposal for a study of the operation of the UN Trusteeship system in Micronesia, which she considered was 'an excellent example of the vulnerability of strategic islands to foreign conquerors.'

Sheila arriving on Truk Island, Micronesia

Sheila wrote: 'These three archipelagos, (the Marshalls, the Carolines, and the Marianas), have been occupied in whole, or in part, by a succession of different powers - Spain, Germany, Japan and the USA. The Spaniards and the Germans were mainly interested in trade and commercial prospects, which proved to be modest. But Japan had greater ambitions. She declared war on Germany - a country with which she had no quarrel - in 1914 and immediately dispatched naval squadrons to occupy the islands. In 1917 she reached an understanding with Britain, France and the Soviet Union that she should retain their possession and her claim was legitimatized at the Paris Peace Settlement in 1920 when the islands were designated as a mandated territory of the newly established League of Nations to be administered by Japan as an integral part of her empire.

This status was soon regarded as unsatisfactory however, since mandated territories remained under the tenure of the League and its terms included demilitarization. Japan then withdrew from the League in 1933 and strongly fortified the islands. Her administration was increasingly secretive. No foreign ships were allowed to fuel there, or make courtesy visits. The reason became clear on 7 December 1941 since a part of the Japanese fleet whose aircraft bombed Pearl Harbor, was based on Palau, the most western group of islands in the territory. The United States immediately entered the Second World War. The islands were particularly at risk because they straddled the sea routes between the Philippines and the Hawaiian islands, which were to become the centre for the Pacific war. In 1944 the Americans invaded Palau and took over the islands after a horrendous battle in which the Japanese defenders fought to the last man. (Total loss of life: 13,600 Japanese and 1,950 Americans.)

On 6 August 1945 the first atom bomb was dropped on Hiroshima, followed three days later by a second bomb on Nagasaki. The attacks were both made from Tinian a small island in the Northern Marianas, which had been taken over by American forces in 1944. The Japanese Emperor accepted the Potsdam Declaration on 14 August and the Japanese General Umezu signed the surrender documents on the US battleship, *Missouri*, on 2 September. The war was over, but US forces remained in temporary occupation of the Territory of the Pacific Islands.

Meanwhile in Washington there was strong pressure within the US Government, particularly the navy, in favour of claiming outright possession of the islands which had proved to be of such strategic importance and which they had won at so much human cost. But since President Roosevelt and Churchill had declared in the Atlantic charter that they 'sought no territorial aggrandisement' the United States finally opted instead for amendments to the Trusteeship articles in the UN Charter then being drafted, which made provision for Strategic Trust Territories. It would be the duty of the administering authority in this case, 'to ensure that the Trust Territory shall play its part in the maintenance of international peace and security.' (Art. 84 of the UN

Charter.) It would thus report to the Security Council instead of the General Assembly. (The former allows a right of veto to the Permanent Members.)

The United States became the fourth foreign power to take over the Territory and was much the most successful. They were faced with a disastrous situation. The Palauan islands, in particular had been devastated. Schools were closed and medical treatment was almost non-existent. There was no trade and a lack of food. Many of the islanders had been displaced from their homes and fishing garounds.

Palau, Micronesia

For some time after its occupation by the US armed forces it was administered by the US Department of the Navy. In 1951, however, responsibility was passed to the Department of the Interior. In 1965 the first elected Congress of Micronesia was convened and from then on following a series of referenda, local governments were established in the Federated States of Micronesia, the Marshall Islands, the Northern Mariana Islands and Palau. The American administration of the Trust Territories has lasted forty-seven years and is now coming to an end. The Federated States of Micronesia, the Marshall Islands, and the Northern Mariana Islands have already become independent and joined the United Nations.'(Palau, after several referenda, became a sovereign state in 1994.)

Sheila represented the United Kingdom on six Visiting Missions to the islands and was Chairman of two of them. Each visit lasted about five or six weeks and the Missions travelled extensively, covering a wide selection of islands each time. She was also President of the Trusteeship Council for the year 1979. This was a great honour and for which, I imagine, she was awarded the OBE. She came home to receive this from the Queen and my mother and I went to Buckingham Palace to see her receive her award. It was a proud occasion. She curtseyed very well, thanks perhaps to Madame Vacani's tuition before her presentation, so many years before. She told us that after they had been instructed by the officials as to how to walk backwards, curtsey, etc., she heard two senior army officers chatting together and saying they were thankful not to be women as they only needed to bow!

The visiting Missions consisted usually of two members of the five Permanent Members of the United Nations representing France and Great Britain. Neither China nor Russia was interested and the United States as Administrator of the region, was not eligible. Thus, in 1979 when Sheila was Chairwoman, Mr. Duque of France and four members of the Secretariat accompanied them to observe the referendum on the Draft constitution of the Marshall Islands. This is her report: 'The Mission arrived in Majuro, the District Centre of the Marshall Islands on 25 February in time to observe the final stages. We left on 7 March. Unfortunately we lacked both the time and the human resources to cover as much of the Territory as we would have wished. In particular we regretted not visiting more of the outer islands. Lack of transport was an additional complication, since the inter-island ships were being used at the time to convey the ballot boxes to and from the outlying islands and travel by sea was particularly difficult to arrange. However, by dividing into two teams for part of the visit, the Mission was able to observe the casting of votes and the subsequent count in the two main population centres of Majuro and Ebeye which together account for approximately two thirds of the registered voters.' (Sheila told me that travelling was on some occasions, very primitive in small aircraft, in helicopters, whose pilots gaily flew over huge sharks to point them out to her, and once before they could land, a herd of pigs had to be removed from the runway.)

'The terms of reference of the Visiting Mission...directed us to observe the referendum including the campaign and polling arrangements, the casting of votes, the closure of voting, the counting of the ballots and the declaration of the results of the referendum. To the extent that its primary purpose permitted, the Mission was required also to obtain first-hand information on political, economic and social developments in the Marshall Islands.... In particular, we believed the Trusteeship Council would wish to satisfy itself that the voters understood what they were voting about and that the referendum was conducted fairly and in accordance with democratic principles. With this objective in mind the

Mission organized public meetings wherever it went. We also made ourselves available to any individuals or small groups who wished to speak to us. We had announced our readiness to do this over the radio. We attended public meetings before and after the referendum organized by both supporters and opponents of the Constitution. We also held restricted meetings with the political leaders of both groups....in addition of course, we considered every complaint raised by one side or the other and referred these to the Election Commissioner. The latter promptly investigated all such complaints and took corrective action.'

As there were so many islands, getting polling booths to them could be very difficult and in some places, such as on Majuro Atoll, mobile units were used. Ballot boxes were taken around by car or boat, supervised by a member of the election board. Sheila told me that one tiny island had only three eligible voters and the ballot box was under a lone palm tree! Sheila was dedicated to the welfare of Micronesia and this is endorsed not only by her colleagues, but also by the other members of the Visiting Missions and many of its peoples. When she was elected as 46th President on 21 March 1979 the outgoing President, M. Brochenin of France said (in an interpretation from the French), I know that we have in Miss Harden a person particularly qualified to guide our work. Sheila Harden has been concerned with Micronesian affairs for many years already and she has a long experience and extensive knowledge of the problems of the Territory. I am convinced that with her charm and her in-depth understanding of Micronesian affairs she will lead this forty-sixth session of the Trusteeship Council to a successful conclusion.' In the following May Mr. Petree of the United States said, 'your distinguished participation in this body dates back to 1975 and you served as Vice-President and Acting President of the Council during the past year. Particularly notable has been your sincere interest in the welfare of the people of Micronesia and the careful attention you have paid to the work of the Council.' As I have mentioned before, even the Russian delegate spoke of her with warmth.

Once Sheila told me how she had persuaded a Russian delegate to accept a point during a discussion that the British delegates had realized they would not like. Soon after they had convened Sheila had brought up some matter, which the Russians were agitated about, but which did not particularly cause Britain concern, and gracefully conceded the point.

Then later when the really important disagreement came up, the Russians accepted it without demur. I expect this is the way diplomacy works, but it was amusing for me to hear.

Her Presidency of the Trusteeship Council and her position twice as Chairwoman of the Visiting Missions to Micronesia was the culmination of Sheila's career. She was only the second woman to become its President. She was asked to stay on an extra year after her retirement date in 1980 to chair the Visiting Mission in that summer. Finally after she had officially retired in January 1981, she was recalled to go yet again to Micronesia for a Trusteeship visit during the Falklands War, when the other British diplomats in New York were too busy. It was during her year as President that Pope John Paul visited the United Nations and Sheila had an audience with him. She was much struck by his charisma and his interest in her work.

21

Epilogue

After Sheila retired she accepted an invitation from Lord Hunt of Tanworth, strongly backed by her last ambassador, Tony Parsons, to become Director of the David Davies Memorial Institute of International Studies. This Institute was formed in 1951 to commemorate and continue the work of David Davies (1880-1944), who in 1932 became Lord Davies of Llandinam. He was a notable Welsh philanthropist, who began his campaign for peace in 1919. He founded the world's first Chair of International Politics at Aberystwyth, thus starting a new discipline, which is read in universities the world over. It laid particular emphasis on the promotion of peace and understanding of the League of Nations.

However, the end of the 1920s had convinced David Davies that the League was incapable of preventing a recurrence of war. He therefore began to campaign for an impartial tribunal to settle international disputes, together with an International Police Force to carry out and if necessary impose its decisions: a forerunner of the United Nations. With the outbreak of war, Lord Davies turned his attention to the future of Europe. In his book *A Federated Europe* he stressed the need for a union not simply of governments but of peoples, with the United States serving as a model for Europe. The founding Charter of his Memorial Institute sets out a wide-ranging brief, 'to advance and promote...international relations in the political, economic, legal, social, educational and other fields.'

'Sheila took up the post of Director of the David Davies Institute in 1984 and was a most hardworking and enthusiastic head of the Institute for eleven years,' wrote John Sankey. ' Eight major studies were published under her direction - just to mention some of them: *Small is Dangerous* on the problems of Micro States (naturally after all Sheila's times in Micronesia), *To Loose the Bands of Wickedness* on international intervention in Human Rights, and *The Conscience of the World* on the influence of non-governmental organizations, as well as studies on South Africa, Antarctica and Terrorism. Many distinguished speakers accepted her invitation to give the Institute's Annual Memorial Lecture, including the then Crown Prince of Jordan; Abba Eban; Garret Fitzgerald; and Maurice Strong.'

I now had retired from the Oxford University Press. But I soon had a new job offered to me by the Press. I was asked to become one of some forty proof-readers for the second edition of *The Oxford English Dictionary*. This monumental dictionary, first undertaken by the Press in 1879 under Queen Victoria, was becoming increasingly out of date, as so many new words from America, the old Empire and elsewhere had become part of the accepted language. Indeed there were already four huge supplements. The Delegates therefore decided it was necessary to produce a second edition which was to be computerized, so that even newer words could be added easily, also scholars could find all the words, perhaps, of Anglo-Saxon origin, which they might need for their research or other such projects. I was very proud to have ended my publishing career on such a project, even though I was only a small cog in the enterprise.

We were initially sent every month about forty pages of computer set copy, without additions, to proof- read against a Xerox of the original dictionary. This part was rather dull work, as three or four different readers had already read it and so one was pleased to find a missing comma! It was also very hard on one's eyes, as the dictionary is printed in very small type, in three columns, and the illustrative quotations, which are probably its most important feature, are often in even more minuscule type and often not only in italics but also in foreign languages. It contained 414,825 headwords and nearly two million illustrative quotations. One then sent back the corrected manuscript and a week later a new set arrived. When the entire dictionary had been proofread, all the new words and those already in the Supplements were incorporated and the whole process began again. This part of the work was much more difficult and so also more interesting, as there were now a great many mistakes. Whole chunks of texts one would find out of order and these had to be rearranged, with computer instructions. Finally I with I suppose twenty-five other readers, was asked to take one letter section (in my case the letter L) and capitalize all those words that should be written with a capital. For instance, Lady Day, referring to the Virgin should be printed with a capital L, while the flower lady's smock is written in lower case.

During these years Sheila and I spent many holidays abroad, often staying with friends Sheila had made, of varying nationalities besides her former British colleagues, whilst she was in New York. Thus we went to Ankara (Turkey), staying with Solmuz and Tewfik Unaydin, (Solmuz was now Turkish Minister for War and her husband a retired ambassador.) They drove us to the fabulous underground cities near Göreme in Cappadocia. Here during the Dark Ages when Tartar hordes were roaming Anatolia, whole villages would descend (when their sentries reported enemy forces), by secret passages underground, where they had constructed complete cave cities and where they would live undetected for a year at a time, until the enemy moved elsewhere.

We also stayed with the Swedish ambassador and his wife the Örns, first at their lovely house on the Rhine, (when he was at Bonn) and later in Rome when he was accredited to the Holy See. This was fascinating as Torsten was able to take us in to the Vatican City to see the gardens, which were not open to the public. Also strangely enough the Vatican City has a beautiful couturier shop, which can be used by diplomats and their wives, but is not much use to the nuns who look after the Pope, who are the main females there. No woman is allowed to sleep within the walls of the Vatican, even the sisters, who look after the Pope.

The Easter following Sheila's retirement we were invited to Egypt by Eric Duchêne, a Belgian diplomat, who had been a friend of hers in New York. He lived in a delightful house with a beautiful garden. An Englishman like so many of our countrymen a passionate gardener, had formerly owned it. Eric was always being asked the names of the flowers and he went around with Sheila (not me as I can hardly tell a rose from a buttercup!) writing down their names to impress future visitors. We also went up the Nile to visit Karnak and the Tombs of the Kings. Eric shortly before had had a very lucky escape from assassination. He was about to accompany his ambassador, then the doyen of the Egyptian diplomatic corps, to an official parade in honour of President Sadat when the Belgian mail arrived. His ambassador said to him regretfully, 'I'm sorry Eric but I'm afraid you will have to remain behind and sort all this out.' An hour later there was a frantic telephone call saying that the President had been shot and the Belgian ambassador sitting beside him, had been very severely wounded. Eric dashed to the scene and organized his ambassador's evacuation by air to a military hospital in Germany, where his life was saved. (Undoubtedly he would have died in an Egyptian hospital at that time. They may be better now.)

Before going to Cairo we had visited Jordan. We had been given an introduction to the Crown Prince (the brother of the late King Hussein). We probably would not have bothered his secretary, had we not had great difficulty finding a room at Petra, which we were most anxious to visit. At that time tourism was in its infancy in Jordan and Petra boasted only one fairly primitive hotel, cut into a cave in the side of the mountains. To our dismay we discovered all the rooms were taken, as it happened to be the combined Orthodox and Roman Easter, so we did ring Prince Hassan's office and invited his secretaries for a drink. They asked if the Prince could do anything for us? ' Could they possibly put in a word for us with the Petra hotel?' we asked. Royal influence worked wonders and presumably, someone was dislodged from a room and we were treated with great honour during our visit! Later Sheila did meet the Prince when he came to London where he gave a lecture at the David Davies Institute. They had the official dinner at the Athenaeum Club and Sheila had been rather upset that the food had been somewhat indifferent and apologized to the Prince. 'Don't worry', he answered, 'I enjoyed it, as it reminded me of my old school dinners!' (Harrow cuisine)

We hired a car in Amman and drove off to see the country. I remember a lovely picnic on the hill above Madaba, where Moses is reputed to have gazed down on the Promised Land, and where a delightful Jordanian family shared a meal with us. We somehow talked without any of us knowing a word of each other's language. The only contretemps was on the way back when I had a puncture in the seething market place in Amman. I was appalled but I need not have worried. We were immediately surrounded by a friendly crowd: two students attacked the wheel, an old white-bearded man held up the traffic with the aid of two small boys, and the wheel was changed in a matter of minutes. Of course I tipped them but it was all done in a spirit of helpfulness towards strangers and the Islamic code of helping women in distress.

Former colleagues of Sheila's were equally hospitable towards us during these years and we had a wonderful holiday with the Sankeys, when he was High Commissioner in Tanzania. Not only did they take us to the Game Reserve, and entertain us in Dar-es-Salaam, but flew us across to Zanzibar. We also stayed both with them and later with a successor, Nigel Williams when they were serving as British Permanent Representatives to the UN in Geneva.

For ten consecutive years we spent very happy weeks in October helping not very efficiently, to pick grapes at the *vendemmia* with our friends the Elleses at their lovely eighteenth-century villa, not far from Lucca. This had formerly been a hunting lodge and has a marvellous view across the Tuscan mountains. There were always charming fellow guests and it was more like a house party than work. Indeed we never seemed to start picking grapes until about eleven. We stopped *pronto* at twelve for lunch, beginning again from 4 until 6pm. After that we sipped the wine from the previous years and had wonderful conversations!

Sheila and I had both been separately to the Holy Land in former years, but the most memorable visit to the Church of the Holy Sepulchre was in the nineties. We had gone on a Car Hirekibbutz trip. This meant that one stayed on a kibbutz, but in their hotel not working the land! Our arrival was rather fraught with problems. I had arranged to pick up the car at the airport of Tel Aviv. By the time we arrived it was close to midnight. I was just handed the keys and then the attendant disappeared. There we were in the dark in an unknown country, with the traffic directions in Hebrew, no promised maps, and a strange car. I drove around the empty parking lot to get the feel of the car and to see where the lights turned on and then set out for Jerusalem. I knew our first kibbutz was off the Jerusalem road. We soon got lost and when I asked the way, I was told that I might be a terrorist! I never drove in Israel at night again.

On Maundy Thursday we went into the Old City and asked at the French Information desk whether the Church of the Holy Sepulchre was open that day. A very helpful assistant said that if we did not mind being locked in the church for three hours, there was a special service for Maundy Thursday, which we could attend. We decided it was a chance not to be missed. All the tourists were turned out of the Church.

Normally it is so packed that you have to fight your way through the crowds, now there were only about twenty lay people prepared to stay. First the Arab protectors of the Church arrived. They have had this honour since the days of the Crusades. They leaned a long ladder against the vast doors. After we and the procession headed by the Catholic Archbishop of Jerusalem and followed by monks had entered, the descendants of the Saracens climbed the ladder and hammered bolts through the iron rings which secured the doors. We were locked in. We walked through the dimly lit cathedral to its very centre, where the Empty Tomb is to be found. The first part of the service was the washing of the monks' feet by the archbishop. Then we lay people were allowed to enter in turn to kiss the floor of the Tomb. Then the monks sang the *Tenebrae* while the candles, all except the one in the Empty Tomb, were put out. It was a long and very cold three hours, as Sheila and I were only wearing cotton frocks, but it was a tremendously moving experience with the wonderful singing and the quietness.

....

Sheila in a field of lavender in Provence.

A Tale of Two Sisters ended when Sheila died very peacefully as she had lived, on 13 July 1999. She was holding my hand as her pulse just stopped. At her funeral at St. Stephen's, Rochester Row, her friend and colleague, John Sankey ended his address with these moving words: 'Her life has thus been one of happiness, achievement and fulfillment. Her humour, her kindness, her interest in people - wherever they came from and whoever they were, her virtues of modesty and humility (to use two old-fashioned words which those who knew Sheila will instantly recognize) endeared her to us all......

We shall miss her deeply, none more than Anne. But we can be sure that for Sheila the gates of Heaven were ready and open to welcome her. May her soul rest in peace.'

Acknowledgements

I am grateful to so many people who have helped me author this biography/autobiography of my sister, Sheila, and myself. First David Jenkinson, without whom I would never have been able to manage the computer, for giving up so much of his time to show me how to use it. To the librarians at the Imperial War Museum, the Army Museum, and Peter Bunsey of the Foreign and Commonwealth library, who found me the relevant documents of Sheila's speeches at The United Nations. They were so kind and patient. To John Sankey, Sheila's colleague and friend, who gave the very moving address at her funeral, which I have quoted.

I am also very much indebted to the following:
Robin Byatt, who was with Sheila in Micronesia, The late Sir Reginald Hibbert, who gave me information about Ulan Bator. My cousins, David O'Brien who very kindly scanned my photographs and Patrick Carswell - Moore who gave me the information about his and his mother's escape from Burma. And to countless other friends who have encouraged and helped me.

During the writing of this manuscript, I consulted the following books, sometimes using short extracts from them with appropriate credits. I would very much appreciate any oversight, error or omission being reported to my publisher.

Old Friends: New Enemies, Vol.2. By A.J. Marder (1981-1990, OUP)
A History of the British Cavalry 1816-1916, By the Marquess of Anglesey
IRD; origins and Establishment of the Foreign Office Information Research Department, 1946-48.(Historians in Library and Records Department of the Foreign and Commonwealth Office.)
Memoirs, by J.R.A. Oldfield
The Causes and Courses of the Second World War, By Peter Calvocoressi.(2nd ed.1989, Viking Press)
May 1942 Trip out of Burma, By Kathleen Learmond *Tigris Gunboats*, By Wilfrid Nunn. (1932, Andrew Melrose) *Code Breakers in the Far East*, By Alan Shipp. (1989, OUP) *Wings of the Dawning*, By Arthur Banks, (1997, Harold Martin & Redman: extracts from *The Diary of Len Birchall*.
War with Japan: 1 & 2, Ministry of Defence (Navy) (1995, HMSO) *War at Sea: 1939-1945*, By S.W Roskill (1954-1961, HMSO)
The Second World War. Vol.2. By Winston S. Churchill. (1948-1954, Cassell)
The Most Dangerous Moment, by M. Tomlinson, (Kimber 1976) *A Book of Readings on Micronesian History*, Edited by F. X Hexel and M.L. Berg. (1979, Saipan) *Queen Victoria's Little Wars*, By Byron Farwell. (Allen Lane, 1973)
Bay of Bengal Pilot (9th ed. 1953)
A Diary of the Indian Mutiny, By Anne Harden (*Notes and Queries*. August 1955)
Report of the United Nations Visiting Mission to observe the Referendum on the Draft Constitution of the Marshall Islands, Trust Territory of the Pacific Islands, March 1979 (T/1805). United Nations. Also (T/PV.1484. 16, T/PV. 1484. 21, T/PV.1496.12)
Election of the President and Vice-President, 21 March 1979. (United Nations, 1979)
New York Times, (24.4.1964 & 24.8.1971)
Star Journal (29.4.1964)
Salt Horse. A Naval Life. By Rear Admiral R.L Fisher.
A Talk on the BBC,1944. By Admiral Sir James Somerville.

Illustrations

1	Henry Angelo's Fencing Academy	4
2	The Grand Harbour, Malta	16
3	Fulpmes	24
4	Innsbruck and the Nordkette	29
5	Coastal scene in Ceylon	37
6	Pellew House, Trincomalee.	42
7	The Iron Gate, Sigiriya, Ceylon	44
8	IJN *Isokase* that picked up Birchall's crew after the Zeros had shot them down on 4 April *(Courtesy Air Cdre Birchall)*	57
9	Map showing the Japanese attacks on Ceylon, April 1942 *(Courtesy of the late Michael Tomlinson)*	62
10	The Taj Mahal	72
11	My father, Commander G.E.Harden, DSO, RN	78
12	The Citadel and the old Admiralty building *(Courtesy Christine Ottewill)*	83
13	Ely House, Dover Street, London	104
14	Sheila behind Sir Patrick Dean, the British ambassador, at the United Nations.	114
15	Sheila meeting the descendant of Christian Fletcher on board a replica of HMS *Bounty* in New York Harbor for the World Fair	119
16	The grizzly bear we met on a path in Glacier National Park.	126
17	My mother, Sheila, and me at the Columbia Glacier, Canada, where the rivers flow to the Atlantic, Pacific, and Arctic Oceans.	127
18	Pacific area map showing the Micronesian Islands.	128
19	Sheila arriving on Truk Island, Micronesia	129
20	Palau, Micronesia	131
21	Sheila in a field of lavender in Provence	140

Printed in the United States
725900001B